P9-ECI-589

Download Forms on Nolo.com

You can download the forms in this book at:

 www.nolo.com/back-of-book/SMLLC.html

We'll also post updates whenever there's an important change to the law affecting this book—as well as articles and other related materials.

More Resources
from Nolo.com

 Legal Forms, Books, & Software
Hundreds of do-it-yourself products—all written in plain English, approved, and updated by our in-house legal editors.

 Legal Articles
Get informed with thousands of free articles on everyday legal topics. Our articles are accurate, up to date, and reader friendly.

 Find a Lawyer
Want to talk to a lawyer? Use Nolo to find a lawyer who can help you with your case.

NOLO
LAW for ALL

⚖ NOLO The Trusted Name
(but don't take our word for it)

"In Nolo you can trust."
THE NEW YORK TIMES

"Nolo is always there in a jam as the nation's premier publisher of do-it-yourself legal books."
NEWSWEEK

"Nolo publications… guide people simply through the how, when, where and why of the law."
THE WASHINGTON POST

"[Nolo's]… material is developed by experienced attorneys who have a knack for making complicated material accessible."
LIBRARY JOURNAL

"When it comes to self-help legal stuff, nobody does a better job than Nolo…"
USA TODAY

"The most prominent U.S. publisher of self-help legal aids."
TIME MAGAZINE

"Nolo is a pioneer in both consumer and business self-help books and software."
LOS ANGELES TIMES

2nd Edition

Nolo's Guide to Single-Member LLCs

How to Form and Run Your Single-Member Limited Liability Company

Attorney David M. Steingold

DRIFTWOOD PUBLIC LIBRARY
801 SW HWY. 101
LINCOLN CITY, OREGON 97367

2ND EDITION	OCTOBER 2019
Book & Cover Design	SUSAN PUTNEY
Proofreading	ROBERT WELLS
Index	SONGBIRD INDEXING SERVICES
Printing	BANG PRINTING

Names: Steingold, David M., author.
Title: Nolo's guide to single-member LLCs : how to form and run your
    single-member limited liability company / Attorney David M. Steingold.
Description: Second edition. | Berkeley, California : Nolo, 2019. | Includes
    index. |
Identifiers: LCCN 2019017901 (print) | LCCN 2019020101 (ebook) | ISBN
    9781413326963 (ebook) | ISBN 9781413326956 (pbk.)
Subjects: LCSH: One-person corporations--United States--Popular works. | Sole
    proprietorship--United States--Popular works. | Private companies--United
    States--Popular works. | One-person corporations--United
    States--Management--Popular works. | Sole proprietorship--United
    States--Management--Popular works. | Private companies--United
    States--Management--Popular works.
Classification: LCC KF1380 (ebook) | LCC KF1380 .S74 2019 (print) | DDC
    346.73/0668--dc23
LC record available at https://lccn.loc.gov/2019017901

This book covers only United States law, unless it specifically states otherwise.
Copyright © 2016, 2019 by Nolo. All rights reserved. The NOLO trademark is registered
in the U.S. Patent and Trademark Office. Printed in the U.S.A.

No part of this publication may be reproduced, stored in a retrieval system, or transmitted
in any form or by any means, electronic, mechanical, photocopying, recording, or otherwise
without prior written permission. Reproduction prohibitions do not apply to the forms
contained in this product when reproduced for personal use. For information on bulk
purchases or corporate premium sales, please contact the Special Sales Department.
Call 800-955-4775 or write to Nolo, 950 Parker Street, Berkeley, California 94710.

Please note

We believe accurate, plain-English legal information should help you solve
many of your own legal problems. But this text is not a substitute for
personalized advice from a knowledgeable lawyer. If you want the help of a
trained professional—and we'll always point out situations in which we think
that's a good idea—consult an attorney licensed to practice in your state.

About the Author

David M. Steingold is a private attorney currently based in Michigan. His practice covers multiple areas including business law. He has been an author for Nolo since 2012.

Table of Contents

Appendixes

Introduction:
Your Single-Member LLC Guide

It's a great time to be the sole owner of a small business. That's because changes in business laws have made the single-member limited liability company (SMLLC) an option in every state. In addition, when Congress passed the Tax Cuts and Jobs Act at the end of 2017, it included a new deduction for people who earn money through pass-through entities like SMLLCs. For SMLLC owners, the deduction could equal up to 20% of their SMLLC income.

This book will give you an overview of what is required to create and operate an SMLLC. The first chapter provides a general explanation of what an SMLLC is and why it may well be the best choice for your small business. Subsequent chapters cover things like formation, taxation, financing, protection from personal liability, and record keeping. Among other matters, this book will tell you:

- what forms and documents you need to create an SMLLC
- how to initially fund an SMLLC
- what your options are for managing an SMLLC
- how to prepare taxes for an SMLLC
- what forms and documents you have to file once your SMLLC is up and running
- what kinds of records you need to maintain for your SMLLC
- how an SMLLC will protect you in the event your business is sued
- what you need to do to maintain limited liability protection for your SMLLC, and
- what liability issues apply specifically to SMLLCs.

Throughout the book you'll find tips, examples, and sample documents that help clarify the most important points.

This book strives to be both relatively compact and reasonably comprehensive. However, you may have additional questions or there may be issues specific to your situation that are not covered here. If so, you may want to consult with a legal or tax expert. Expert advice can help ensure that an SMLLC is the best choice for your business and that you have considered all the legal and tax issues that might apply to your particular situation. If you decide you want to form an SMLLC but you don't want to do the paperwork and filings yourself, Nolo has an online LLC formation service that will take care of everything for you, including creating a customized SMLLC operating agreement.

Whether you have already taken the plunge and created your SMLLC or are still deciding whether an SMLLC is right for you, this book has all the essential information you'll need about what it takes to form, own, and operate an SMLLC.

Get Updates and Forms Online

Check the Nolo website at:

www.nolo.com/back-of-book/SMLLC.html

There is a page dedicated to this book where you can download forms from the Appendix and check for updates to the information in this book.

LLCs and Business Structure Basics

ingle-owner businesses have always existed in this country. Historically, they have been structured either as sole proprietorships or single-shareholder corporations, both of which have certain drawbacks for small single-owner businesses. However, since the late 1990s, it's become possible to organize these businesses as SMLLCs, a type of business entity which, for a single-owner business, has some advantages over both the sole proprietorship and the corporation. This chapter reviews those advantages and explains how organizing your business as an SMLLC may be the best option for you.

> **TIP**
>
> **Every business has a legal structure.** This includes everyone from a college student you pay to mow your lawn to an international telecommunications company you pay for cellphone service. The telecommunications company has likely organized as some type of formal business entity—either a corporation or an LLC. The college student, on the other hand, probably has not taken the trouble to file special documents to create a business entity, in which case he or she would be considered a sole proprietor (the default structure for a single-owner business).

Why an LLC?

Forming a limited liability company has become an increasingly popular way to create a formal legal structure for a small business. An LLC selectively combines some of the most desirable features of older, more traditional business structures like corporations, partnerships, and sole proprietorships. Those features include the limitation on personal liability that you get with a corporation and the pass-through taxation and flexibility of management that you get with a partnership or sole proprietorship. SMLLCs are LLCs with just one owner and they have the same combination of desirable features as multi-member LLCs. SMLLCs are specifically authorized by statute in every state.

LLCs Can Have Other Advantages

Protection from personal liability generally is considered the most important benefit you get from organizing your single-owner business as an SMLLC. Pass-through taxation and flexibility of management (which also apply to sole proprietorships but not corporations) are two other benefits. However, beyond liability protection, pass-through taxation, and flexible management, LLCs can have other, less commonly discussed benefits. Two worth mentioning are privacy and prestige.

Privacy. There are methods you can employ to make it difficult for other people to know who actually owns your SMLLC. An LLC created and operated using these methods is sometimes called an anonymous LLC. At a minimum, the methods for creating and maintaining an anonymous LLC include using a separate company to act as your business's registered agent, and not listing the name of your LLC's (single) member on the articles of organization or annual reports. Additional steps may be necessary.

These methods are permissible in some states but not others. That's not necessarily a problem because you don't have to organize your SMLLC in the state where you'll actually operate. However, you will have to check around to find a state that has favorable LLC privacy rules. Also, be aware that with an anonymous SMLLC, you'll have expenses that you might otherwise avoid—such as paying someone else to act as your business's registered agent.

Anonymity similar to what you can achieve with an anonymous LLC generally is not available when operating a sole proprietorship.

Prestige. Many people believe that operating as an SMLLC, as opposed to a sole proprietorship, makes a business appear more impressive and reliable. In part, the idea is that if you're taking the time to complete and pay for the initial filings, and then keep up with the ongoing paperwork and fees, people will perceive you as more committed to your business. You'll have to decide for yourself whether this would be true in your particular case. Keep in mind that if you feel you don't need protection from liability, you'll have to balance the value of greater prestige against the initial and ongoing costs associated with having an SMLLC.

Furthermore, with the passage of the Tax Cuts and Jobs Act (TCJA), you may get up to a 20% tax deduction on the income you earn from your SMLLC. The 20% deduction applies to most SMLLC owners, although some limitations apply if you are providing services in fields such as health care, law, or accounting.

Forming an SMLLC can be relatively quick and simple. However, that fact alone shouldn't stop you from wondering why you should give your small business a formal legal structure beyond the default structure of sole proprietorship. It's a good question to ask. Not every small business, and certainly not every one-owner business, needs what an LLC has to offer. As just mentioned, sole proprietorships, too, have pass-through taxation and flexibility of management. Consequently, most business owners, and especially those who are sole owners, consider liability protection as the key issue in deciding whether to form an LLC. This chapter focuses on that particular benefit.

Protection From Personal Liability

If you are the sole owner of a small business and you choose not to give it any legal structure, your business will be considered a sole proprietorship by default. In turn, as a sole proprietorship, your business isn't considered legally separate from you, personally. This means:

- debts for your business are also your own personal debts
- you, personally, are liable for any injuries your business causes to other people, and
- you, personally, are liable for damage your business causes to anyone else's property.

By contrast, if you organize your one-person business as an SMLLC, you generally will not have personal liability for debts, injuries, or damage caused by your business.

So, with the liability issue in mind, what kinds of one-owner businesses can benefit by being structured as SMLLCs? The simple answer is: businesses where there is at least a small chance of significant liability. A few examples will make this clearer.

EXAMPLE: Rosa has a degree in computer science. However, for the five years since finishing college she has worked nearly full time as an assistant manager at a retail store. She's glad to be employed, but the job doesn't pay enough and she never has a chance to use her computer skills. Six months ago, Rosa started doing freelance website development work from her home for several businesses in the state where she lives. Rosa does this as "work-for-hire" so that her clients own what she produces. On an hourly basis, Rosa earns a lot more from the freelance work than she gets from her assistant manager job. However, Rosa only has about a dozen hours of freelance work each week and it's not clear if she'll be able to get more work. Rosa has thought about formally setting up her Web development business as an SMLLC. However, she isn't sure she is ready to pay the $150 filing fee her state charges to set up an LLC. Rosa already has most of the hardware, software, books, and other supplies she needs to run her freelance operation so there is little chance it will put her deeply into debt. Equally important, because Rosa does most of her work from her own home, at a computer, there is very little chance that her work will lead to someone being injured or someone's property being damaged. Consequently, Rosa reasonably decides that, at least for now, it's not necessary to set up her business as an SMLLC.

EXAMPLE: Two years ago, Robert had a great idea for a new kind of baby stroller. He calls it the Carbo-Lite Carriage. The new design is made out of special lightweight carbon, making it easier than ever for parents to jog with their babies. (It also looks really cool.) After having built some prototypes on his own, and seen some local interest in the product, Robert now wants to hire a couple of part-time employees to help him ramp up production. He also wants to open a small local store to sell the stroller. Robert will need to get loans to make this happen. Up until now, Robert has thought of the stroller mainly as a pet project and has not given his "business" any legal structure. However, he recently spoke with an attorney who suggested that Robert set up Carbo-Lite Carriages as an SMLLC. As the attorney explained, Robert's business will have various possible areas of liability:

- an employee could get hurt while working for Robert

- a customer or a customer's child might get hurt in the store, for example by slipping and falling
- even though the stroller is very sturdy, there is a chance that a customer or child might be hurt because of some unexpected defect
- while Robert believes his product is unique, it's nevertheless possible that someone else could bring an intellectual property claim, for example for patent infringement, and
- it's possible that, in spite of the initial interest Robert has seen, the stroller won't ultimately sell well enough to be profitable and Robert would find he couldn't pay back his business loans or other business debts.

Because of all these possible areas of liability, Robert takes his attorney's advice and sets up Carbo-Lite Carriages, LLC, as a single-member limited liability company.

If you don't establish your one-owner business as an SMLLC and instead leave it as a sole proprietorship, you'll still have to pay taxes on business income, keep records for the business, and do nearly everything else you'd have to do if the business were an SMLLC. The most important difference between keeping your one-owner business as a sole proprietorship and forming it as an SMLLC is that, if you leave it as a sole proprietorship, you'll leave yourself open to personal liability.

TIP

Every state has an LLC Act that lays out the state requirements for an LLC. If you're ever wondering about the official rules for an LLC in your state, your state's LLC Act is a good place to look for an answer. You can find each state's LLC Act online by searching on the state name and "LLC Act." Answers to many state-specific LLC questions also can be found on each state's secretary of state (or equivalent office) website.

The "Novelty" of Single-Member LLCs

Both in general terms and also when specifically compared to multi-member LLCs, SMLLCs are a little unusual. Distinctive aspects of SMLLCs are apparent when it comes to basic LLC matters like operating agreements, member meetings and resolutions, personal liability, and taxation. In some cases, these distinctions result from the fact that many of the structural elements of LLCs are adapted from laws and rules for corporations, and those laws and rules frequently assume that businesses are owned and operated by more than one person.

Operating agreements. Where corporations have bylaws to help guide a group of directors, LLCs usually have operating agreements to guide multiple members. More specifically, two key purposes of an operating agreement for a multi-member LLC are to give all the LLC members a written document to refer to in case of an internal disagreement about the company, and to describe how different members will share in the company's profits. However, with an SMLLC, which has just one member, there is no possibility of a disagreement among members and no issue of sharing profits. This doesn't mean that you shouldn't have an operating agreement for an SMLLC; it just means that the document may serve a somewhat different purpose than for a multi-member LLC. Operating agreements are covered in detail in the chapter on forming your SMLLC.

Meetings and resolutions. A similar novelty for SMLLCs relates to member meetings and resolutions. Just as corporations have shareholder and board of directors meetings, multi-member LLCs often provide for member meetings to make business decisions. And, when multi-member LLCs make big decisions, they commonly are documented in the form of resolutions. With SMLLCs, the sole owner has no other members to meet with and may not appear to have the same need to document decisions. Again, this doesn't mean that, even if you don't have meetings, you shouldn't at least document major decisions for an SMLLC. Some of these issues are covered in more detail in the chapters on managing your SMLLC and keeping records for your SMLLC.

Personal liability. SMLLCs are sometimes looked at differently than multi-member LLCs when it comes to liability. In general, certain limits are placed on creditors trying to collect unpaid business debts from LLCs; or, conversely, trying to collect unpaid personal debts from individual LLC members. This might mean a creditor would be prohibited from collecting an unpaid LLC debt from the personal assets of an LLC member. It also might mean that a creditor trying to collect on an LLC member's unpaid personal debt would be blocked from taking control and selling the assets of the LLC. However, in both of these situations, some states provide creditors of SMLLCs with more rights—more access to either personal assets or business assets. These matters are covered in the chapter on liability.

Taxation. SMLLCs are also taxed differently than multi-member LLCs. Both types of LLC are subject to pass-through taxation (meaning the LLC itself doesn't pay taxes on business income, only the individual members do). However, while multi-member LLCs are taxed like partnerships, SMLLCs are taxed as disregarded entities (the same as sole proprietorships). This distinction, along with many other tax issues, is covered in more detail in the chapter on taxation.

Perhaps the ultimate evidence of the novelty of SMLLCs, as well as the slight uncertainty regarding their status, is the fact that by 1996 every state had laws allowing for LLCs but it took until 2003 before the last of the 50 states had updated their laws to specifically allow for SMLLCs. However, once that happened, the owner of an SMLLC formed in any U.S. jurisdiction could feel confident that the company—and its limited liability—would be recognized and respected in every other U.S. jurisdiction.

As you read through this book, it's always useful to keep in mind that SMLLCs in many ways are a special case among LLCs generally.

TIP

Many states have LLC laws based on a model known as the Uniform Limited Liability Company Act (ULLCA). The ULLCA contains both suggested rules and also explanatory comments about those rules. The ULLCA is periodically updated, though any single update usually involves only limited, incremental changes. Apart from your own state's laws, which are the most important place to check for questions about what LLCs can and can't do (and must and must not do), you sometimes can find additional guidance, including about SMLLCs specifically, from the comments in the ULLCA. You can find a copy of the latest version of the ULLCA online if you do a search for "Uniform Limited Liability Company Act."

Business Structures and Personal Liability

While an LLC often is the most sensible legal form for a small business, it isn't the only option. The other main choices are:

- sole proprietorship
- partnership, and
- corporation.

Each of these structures has unique elements. For example, a sole proprietorship can only have one proprietor, but a partnership must have at least two partners. As already mentioned, sole proprietorships and partnerships are not taxed separately from their owners (they are subject to so-called pass-through taxation), but corporations are taxed separately. In addition, there are variations on some of these structures, such as limited partnerships and S corporations.

Main Types of Business Structures				
Type of Structure	Sole Proprietorship	Partnership	LLC	Corporation
Number of Owners	One owner (proprietor) maximum	Minimum of at least two owners (partners)	One owner/ member (SMLLC) or multiple owners/members (multi-member LLC)	One or more owners/share-holders; most states allow one-person corporations
Limited Liability?	No limited liability; sole proprietor is liable for unpaid debts, injuries, and damage	No limited liability; partners are liable for unpaid debts, injuries, and damage	Limited liability; members are protected in cases of unpaid debts, injuries, and damage	Limited liability; shareholders are protected in cases of unpaid debts, injuries, and damage
Taxation	Pass-through taxation; sole proprietor pays taxes on business income as part of personal tax return	Pass-through taxation; partners pay taxes on business income as part of their personal tax returns	Pass-through taxation; members pay taxes on business income as part of their personal tax returns (members can elect to have the LLC taxed as a corporation)	Corporation pays 21% tax on net income and shareholders pay taxes on income they receive from the corporation
Management Flexibility	Flexible management; sole proprietor largely can do what he or she likes	Flexible management; partners largely can do what they like so long as they agree with each other	Flexible management; members largely can do what they like so long as they agree with each other (for SMLLCs, the single member largely can do what he or she likes)	Not so flexible; regular director and shareholder meetings and votes on major decisions required

Main Types of Business Structures (continued)				
Type of Structure	**Sole Proprietorship**	**Partnership**	**LLC**	**Corporation**
Variations	No important variations	Limited Partnerships (LPs) and Limited Liability Partnerships (LLPs) (available mainly to professionals)	Single-member LLCs (LLCs with just one owner/member)	S-type corporations (corporations with pass-through taxation)

With a sole proprietorship, the owner is legally identified with the business and there is no personal liability protection if the business has unpaid debts, harms other people, or damages someone else's property. The same holds true for a general partnership: The individual partners share liability with the business. By contrast, the owners of a corporation (who are the shareholders) are considered separate from the corporation, and generally are not responsible for the corporation's unpaid debts or any harm or damage caused by the corporation.

TIP
In some cases, small business owners can benefit from the special way that corporations are taxed. However, that doesn't automatically mean that the best option in those cases is to form the business as a corporation. Instead, it may make more sense to create an LLC and then elect to have it taxed like a corporation. There are more details in the chapter on taxation.

For small business owners seeking limited liability protection, an LLC usually is the best choice, in part because LLC owners:
- do not have to prepare and file separate taxes for the business apart from their personal tax returns, and

- are not by default required to hold and document regular owner (member) meetings.

However, for some small business owners seeking limited liability, a corporation may be a better choice than an LLC. This is true primarily for businesses that:

- have employees, including employee-owners, and want to provide those employees with the widest possible range of fringe benefits and incentives, and
- want to make it as easy as possible to attract outside investment, particularly through initial public offerings of stock (IPOs).

Unlike LLCs, corporations can offer employee-owners and other employees the widest available range of fringe benefits, such as various benefits related to health care. For employees of corporations, all of these fringe benefits are tax free, and they generally are also tax deductible for the corporation. Some of these same benefits would not be tax free if offered by an LLC to its members. On the other hand, keep in mind that LLC members who actively participate in the business are considered self-employed, and consequently are eligible for the self-employed health insurance deduction offered by the IRS. Therefore, at least when it comes to health insurance, LLC members can deduct 100% of their self-employed health insurance premiums on their personal tax returns. In short, employee fringe benefits, alone, usually aren't enough reason to choose the corporation form over the LLC form.

> **TIP**
> **There are a few basic rules for taking the self-employed health insurance deduction.** Your health insurance policy must be in your own name or the name of your SMLLC. In addition, your business must have a net profit for the year. You typically report that profit on an IRS Schedule C. You enter the amount of the health insurance deduction on your personal Form 1040. For additional details on the deduction, check the instructions for Form 1040 and Schedule C, which are available on the IRS website.

Also unlike LLCs, corporations can offer stock options to prospective employees as an incentive to work for the company. On the other hand, multi-member LLCs can offer LLC memberships to employees as incentives. (Be aware, though, that LLC members are not employees but rather self-employed individuals with rights regarding the running of the LLC that employees don't have.)

Finally, in contrast to LLC ownership, which is based on memberships, corporation ownership is based on shares of stock, so corporations can offer potential investors stock in the company, including different classes of stock with different rights. This is often more attractive than LLC memberships, particularly to public investors. However, most small business owners who are considering establishing their businesses as LLCs are not, and never will be, interested in taking their businesses public with IPOs.

TIP

If you want, you can change an LLC into a corporation. This is known as converting your business entity. In the majority of states, it has become easier in recent years to do entity conversions because of new streamlined procedures. Be aware, though, that—as mentioned above and discussed more fully in the chapter on taxation—a corporation is taxed differently than a typical SMLLC. Also, there's information in Chapter 4 regarding the reverse process—converting from a corporation to an LLC.

CAUTION

The rules mentioned here are for standard C corporations, not for so-called S corporations. S corporations are a special type of closely-held corporation. Among other things, S corporations can only have one class of stock and a limited number of shareholders. Also, unlike C corporations, S corporations have pass-through taxation (the S corporation itself doesn't pay tax on net business income, only the individual shareholders do). S corporations are discussed in the chapter on taxation.

A more detailed review of each of the main types of business structures is beyond the scope of this book. However, Nolo publishes many books on starting and running all sorts of small businesses. Check *Legal Guide for Starting & Running a Small Business,* by Fred S. Steingold and David M. Steingold, *The Small Business Start-Up Kit,* by Peri Pakroo, and *Form Your Own Limited Liability Company,* by Anthony Mancuso. In addition, if you're uncertain specifically about whether to establish your small business as an LLC or a corporation, check out *LLC or Corporation?* by Anthony Mancuso. ●

Taxation of SMLLCs

L ike pretty much any other business, an SMLLC is subject to federal and state taxes. That means that, at a minimum, you'll have to pay taxes on any profit your business makes. In addition, depending on where your SMLLC is registered, where you do business, whether you have employees, and the type of business you're engaged in, you may also have to pay other kinds of taxes or fees.

Default Pass-Through Tax Treatment

By default, the IRS will treat your SMLLC as what it calls a "disregarded entity." This means that the IRS will not look at your SMLLC as an entity separate from yourself for the purpose of filing tax returns. Instead, just as it would do with a sole proprietorship, the IRS will disregard your SMLLC, and you'll pay taxes for the business as part of your own personal tax returns. Because responsibility for paying income tax on an SMLLC classified as a disregarded entity passes through the SMLLC to you personally, this way of taxing SMLLC profits is called pass-through taxation.

 TIP

You don't need to specify your tax classification with the IRS. Because disregarded entity is the default classification for an SMLLC, you do not need to notify the IRS that you're choosing this classification. The IRS will simply assume this is your choice unless you tell it otherwise. If, however, you want to have your SMLLC classified as a corporation, you will need to make an election with the IRS. (See "Electing Corporation Tax Treatment," below.)

Paying Federal Income Tax

To report and pay federal income tax on your SMLLC's business, you will need to attach Schedule C, *Profit or Loss From Business,* to the personal federal tax return you file with the IRS. You also may need to use Schedule E if your SMLLC is used for rental of real estate. Schedule C contains information about your SMLLC's annual income, expenses, and overall profit or loss. To complete Schedule C, you'll need to have good records of all of the income and expenses associated with your SMLLC. This means you'll need to track bank deposits and keep receipts and records of your SMLLC's business transactions throughout the year. (In addition, if you have a home office, you should keep track of any relevant home expenses, and complete Form 8829, *Expenses for Business Use of Your Home,* that shows how you calculated your home office deduction.)

You attach Schedule C, along with any other required schedules or forms, to your IRS Form 1040, *U.S. Individual Income Tax Return.* The net profit (or loss) that you show on Schedule C is included as part of the total income (or loss) that you report on your personal Form 1040.

> **EXAMPLE:** Marcy has an SMLLC for her part-time, home-based landscape design business. Last year, she earned a total of $30,000 from the business and had expenses totaling $5,000 for new equipment, supplies, and other items. She also earned $50,000 in salary from her part-time job with an architectural firm. Marcy uses Schedule C to show her earnings and expenses from her website design business. She attaches the Schedule C to her personal Form 1040, where she reports and pays taxes on her combined gross income of $75,000 ($25,000 from her landscape design business and $50,000 from her architectural job).

You Must Pay Tax on All Profit (Whether You Distribute It or Not)

As a disregarded entity, if your SMLLC has a net profit for a given year, you're required to pay taxes on that profit, regardless of whether or not you actually distribute that profit to yourself. The IRS doesn't distinguish between cases where an owner of an SMLLC leaves the profits in the company's bank account and those where the owner withdraws the money. Instead, for tax purposes, the IRS assumes all profits are distributed to the SMLLC owner. The IRS takes this approach because it doesn't want SMLLC owners to take different amounts of money out of the business each year in order to lower their annual taxes.

EXAMPLE: Ryan's SMLLC, which manufactures and sells motorcycle accessories, earned $120,000 this year after expenses. Ryan knows he'll need $60,000 next year to buy new equipment and inventory. However, even if he leaves $60,000 in his company account to use next year for business-related purposes, he will have to report and pay tax on the full $120,000.

How Much Money Should You Leave in Your Business?

Since the IRS is going to tax 100% of your SMLLC's profit regardless of how much you actually take out for yourself, you might be inclined to take out all of it, down to the very last penny. However, taking absolutely everything out of your SMLLC generally isn't a good idea—and probably would run afoul of your state's LLC laws. Instead, you should try to balance your personal financial needs with the financial obligations of your business.

On the one hand, you'll want to pay yourself at least enough money to cover your personal tax obligations related to the business—which mainly means income taxes and self-employment taxes. On the other hand, you want to avoid taking so much money out of your company that it can't meet its financial obligations. This is true even if you're temporarily operating at a loss. In most cases, state law requires that you always leave enough money in your business so that it can continue paying its bills. Similarly, you should make sure that at all times your business's assets exceed its liabilities. If you don't follow these rules, and a creditor or an injured person sues you, a court may decide that your business no longer has limited liability, and you, personally, are responsible for any debts or other claims.

The 20% Pass-Through Deduction

As the owner of an SMLLC, your income from the SMLLC will likely be eligible for the 20% pass-through deduction. The deduction was included as part of the Tax Cuts and Jobs Act (TCJA) that was passed at the end of 2017. The TCJA allows owners of pass-through businesses—which includes SMLLCs—to deduct up to 20% of their qualified business income (QBI) from their total taxable income for the year. QBI is the net income or profit that the pass-through business earns for the year. Compared to the taxes paid by people running their businesses as corporations, this can result in substantial savings on federal taxes.

You can only use the 20% deduction if you have an overall profit from your pass-through businesses. For example, if you have two businesses, and one earns $100,000 of QBI, but the other one has a loss of $150,000 of QBI, you will not be entitled to the 20% deduction. Moreover, you must carry over and apply the overall loss of $50,000 in QBI to your taxes for the following year.

The maximum amount of the deduction is 20% of your QBI and that amount cannot exceed 20% of your taxable income. For example, if your only income for the year is $80,000 of QBI and you take the standard deduction ($12,200 in 2019), your total taxable income for the year would be $67,800. Because this is less than your QBI, your deduction would be limited to 20% of $67,800 ($13,560) instead of 20% of $80,000 ($16,000).

If you provide certain services or work in certain trades, the amount of income eligible for this deduction is limited or the amount of the deduction is reduced. The IRS calls these areas of work "specified service trades or businesses" (SSTBs). An SSTB is any trade or business providing services in the fields of:

- health, such as doctors and nurses
- law, such as lawyers and paralegals
- accounting, such as accountants and tax return preparers
- actuarial science
- performing arts
- consulting, such as work done by lobbyists
- athletics, such as athletes, coaches, and managers
- financial services, such as wealth managers and financial advisors
- brokerage services
- investing and investment management
- trading, such as trading securities, and
- any trade or business where the principal asset is the reputation or skill of one or more of its employees, as demonstrated in a variety of ways.

If your SMLLC earns income through a specified service trade or business, and that income exceeds $160,725 for a single taxpayer or $321,400 for a married taxpayer filing jointly (2019), your available deduction will be reduced from the 20% maximum. For more information on the 20% pass-through deduction and the SSTB limitation, check the IRS website.

SMLLC Owners Pay Self-Employment Taxes

As the owner of an SMLLC with the default tax classification of disregarded entity, you are not considered an employee, and income you receive from your company is not considered a salary. Instead, just like a sole proprietor, the IRS considers you to be self-employed, and the income you receive is considered earnings from self-employment. As such, income you receive from your SMLLC is subject to federal self-employment tax.

Self-employment tax is separate from, and in addition to, the tax you pay on your gross income. The federal government taxes most, but not quite all, of a person's income from self-employment. (To be precise, the tax applies to 92.35% of your net earnings from self-employment.) The first $132,900 (2019) of self-employment income is taxed at a rate of 15.3%. This consists of a 12.4% tax for Social Security and a 2.9% tax for Medicare. For earnings from self-employment above $132,900, only the Medicare tax applies. An additional 0.9% Medicare tax applies to self-employed taxpayers whose income exceeds $200,000 ($250,000 if married and filing jointly). As a (perhaps minor) consolation, you can deduct half of the amount of your self-employment tax as a business expense, which lowers your overall federal tax bill.

When it's time to file your annual federal tax return, you'll need to include Schedule SE, *Self-Employment Tax*, with your Form 1040. Schedule SE is the IRS form used to compute and report the amount of your self-employment tax obligation. Some of the information on Schedule SE comes from Schedule C so you'll want to have your Schedule C handy when you work on Schedule SE. Also, keep in mind that if you didn't earn more than $132,900 (2019) from self-employment, and meet a few other conditions, you can use the short form of Schedule SE.

EXAMPLE: After ten years working as an electrical engineer for a large corporation, Tessa starts a part-time business as an engineering consultant to small tech start-ups. She creates an SMLLC and, in its first year, Tessa's new business earns a $20,000 net profit. When Tessa files her taxes, she includes Schedule SE, which shows $20,000 of self-employment income from her SMLLC. She pays 15.3% self-employment tax on that amount ($3,060). She also gets to deduct half the self-employment taxes she paid ($1,530) as a business expense on her Form 1040, which reduces the adjusted gross income she reports for the year (and therefore lowers her overall taxes). Tessa may be entitled to the 20% pass-through deduction on her $20,000 of SMLLC income—but the deduction does not reduce her earnings that are subject to self-employment tax.

You Don't Pay Self-Employment Tax on Passive Income

Owners of SMLLCs engaged in most kinds of business must pay self-employment tax. A key exception is for owners engaged in a passive activity that generates passive income. The IRS defines just two types of passive activity:

- trade or business activities in which you do not materially participate during the year; and
- rental activities, even if you materially participate in them, unless you are a real estate professional.

We won't look at the first type of activity: It would be highly unusual for a person to own an SMLLC engaged in trade or business yet not materially participate in those activities.

The second type of activity, however, is important to keep in mind. Many people use SMLLCs in connection with rental property they own. If you've set up an SMLLC for this purpose, you won't need to pay self-employment tax on your rental income. You will, however, need to report any income (or loss) from your rental property using IRS Schedule E, *Supplemental Income or Loss*. The information on Schedule E ultimately gets carried over to your Form 1040 and is factored into your overall income tax liability.

Unless an SMLLC is reclassified as a corporation for tax purposes, it's generally not possible for the owner of an SMLLC to avoid the requirement to pay self-employment taxes. By contrast, under certain conditions, individual members of some multi-member LLCs can avoid self-employment taxes without reclassification. If reducing or avoiding self-employment taxes is extremely important to you, you may want to check into converting your SMLLC to a multi-member LLC with passive members or a nonmember manager—or, as discussed below, reclassifying your company as an S corporation.

Paying Estimated Taxes

As the sole member of an SMLLC classified as a disregarded entity, the IRS considers you to be a self-employed individual. As such, you are not subject to tax withholding. In other words, unlike an employee, you are not receiving a regular paycheck from an employer who holds back money from your base salary for federal income tax, Social Security, and Medicare. (If you've ever been an employee and looked at your paycheck stub, you've seen these withholdings.) Because no employer is holding back taxes, the IRS requires you to make interim, partial payments of federal income tax and self-employment tax without waiting for you to file your annual tax return. Estimated tax is the method the IRS uses to collect this money.

You make estimated tax payments on a quarterly basis throughout the calendar year. Payments are due by April 15th, June 15th, September 15th, and January 15th. If the 15th of the month falls on a weekend then the due date is the following Monday. Calculating the amount you need to pay each quarter sometimes can be tricky. Often it's useful to use your tax information from the prior year as a general guide. Also, if you find you're paying too little or too much after one or more quarterly payments, you can adjust up or down on later payments. What you want to avoid is paying too little by the time you've made your final estimated tax payment in January: If you underpay by more than $1,000, or pay less than 90% of the total taxes you'll ultimately owe, you'll probably have to pay an underpayment penalty.

Once you've determined how much you owe, making an estimated tax payment is a fairly simple matter of writing a check, attaching it to a Form 1040-ES, *Estimated Tax for Individuals*, and mailing it to the IRS. You can download the forms from the IRS website; they come in dated sets of four, one for each quarterly payment.

> **CAUTION**
>
> **Estimated tax is different for corporations.** If you've elected to have your SMLLC taxed as a traditional corporation, it's the company itself that makes the estimated tax payments, not you individually. To do this, you will use Form 1120-W, *Estimated Tax for Corporations*, instead of Form 1040-ES.

Electing Corporation Tax Treatment

While the default federal tax status for an SMLLC is disregarded entity with pass-through taxation, you do have a choice about how your company is classified with, and taxed by, the IRS. Instead of the default pass-through taxation status, you can elect to have your SMLLC taxed as one of two types of corporation:

- a traditional corporation, officially known as a C corporation (which in this book is referred to simply as a corporation), or
- an S corporation, which is a special type of small, closely-held corporation.

Let's briefly review each type of corporate tax classification.

How to Make the C Corporation Election

You can file an election for corporation tax status at any time after setting up your SMLLC. However, there are limitations on when the election can take effect. Specifically, your corporation tax status must become effective within the 75-day period before the filing date or within 12 months after the filing date. To make the election, complete and file IRS Form 8832, *Entity Classification Election*. The form is fairly simple and mainly involves checking off a few boxes. (In fact, this way of choosing a business's tax status is officially known as "check-the-box.")

Your tax situation will be significantly different if you elect to have your SMLLC taxed as a traditional corporation instead of as a disregarded entity. For example, unlike a disregarded entity:

- a corporation is not subject to pass-through taxation
- the IRS does not consider the owner of a corporation to be self-employed, and
- the IRS does not assume all profits are distributed to the owner each year.

Let's quickly look at each of these points.

No Pass-Through Taxation

A corporation is considered a separate entity from its owners (shareholders) and employees, and is not disregarded by the IRS. As a separate entity, a corporation files its own income tax forms and pays its own taxes each year on its net income. For decades, corporations paid taxes to the IRS at graduated tax rates that ranged (most recently) from 35% at the highest income levels to 15% at the lowest level. The TCJA eliminated the graduated corporate tax rates and imposed a new flat corporate tax rate of 21%. In addition to the 21% federal corporate income tax your SMLLC will owe the IRS, most states also have a corporation income tax. Depending on the state, the tax can range from 4% to 12%.

 CAUTION

No special corporate tax rate for personal service corporations. For many years, personal service corporations (PSCs) were subject to a flat 35% corporate tax rate, regardless of the amount of net profit they earned. Personal service corporations are those providing services in the fields of accounting, actuarial science, architecture, consulting, engineering, health, law, or the performing arts. Under the TCJA, PSCs are now taxed at the same 21% flat rate as other corporations.

No Self-Employment Taxes

If your SMLLC is classified as a corporation, then, in contrast to owning an SMLLC classified as a disregarded entity, the IRS does not consider you to be self-employed and does not automatically assume you receive all of your company's profits. Instead, each year you receive from your company whatever amount of money you choose, and you, personally, are taxed only on that amount. The company is taxed on the remainder at the flat 21% rate. Moreover, you choose how that money comes to you. Generally, this means receiving it either as a dividend or as salary. Other, less common options also exist, such as receiving a bonus over and above a salary or receiving money from the business as a loan. Dividends are taxed differently from salaries, and both methods of receiving money are taxed differently than money from self-employment.

More specifically, a dividend is not a deductible business expense. Therefore, both your SMLLC and you, personally, have to pay taxes on dividend money. In other words, dividend money is subject to double taxation. In contrast to a dividend, a corporation can deduct as a business expense any salary it pays to an employee. Because dividend money is taxed twice but a salary is only taxed once, most SMLLC owners who choose to have their businesses taxed as corporations receive their money as a salary.

Be aware, however, that if you treat yourself as an employee and pay yourself a salary, your SMLLC must follow the same tax rules as any other employer. This includes withholding the required employer taxes, depositing the withheld money in a separate account, and ultimately paying that money to the federal government. It also includes filing a quarterly employer tax return (Form 941) with a quarterly tax payment (this can be done by mail or electronically by using an e-file or electronic funds transfer system).

EXAMPLE: Charlie's SMLLC manufactures and sells shipping boxes. Charlie has elected to have the company taxed as a C corporation. For the most recent tax year, the business had $90,000 in net profits, not including any payments to Charlie. He wanted $60,000 of the money for himself, but didn't want to pay double taxes on it. So, rather than taking a dividend, Charlie paid himself a monthly salary of $5,000. Each month, he made sure to calculate how much his company had to withhold for Social Security, Medicare, and federal income tax, and he put that money in a separate account. Each quarter, he sent the withheld money to the IRS electronically using the Form 941 e-file system. Also, on a quarterly basis, his SMLLC made estimated tax payments using Form 1120-W. At tax time, the company filed a separate tax return to pay taxes at the 21% corporate tax rate on the $30,000 of profit remaining after Charlie's payments to himself. Charlie also reported and paid taxes on the $60,000 annual salary he received on his personal Form 1040.

Electing S Corporation Tax Status

An S corporation, like a typical LLC or sole proprietorship (but unlike a traditional corporation), is a pass-through tax entity. In other words, the responsibility for paying income tax passes through the business to you personally. To elect S corporation tax status, you need to file IRS Form 2553, *Election by a Small Business Corporation*. Just as with a C corporation, you can file an election for S corporation tax status at any time, and, just as with a C corporation, there are limits on when the election can take effect. As with choosing to be taxed as a traditional corporation, electing S corporation tax status means you'll have to file additional tax documents each year, such as Form 1120S, *U.S. Income Tax Return for an S Corporation*.

Since both SMLLCs and S corporations have pass-through taxation, and being taxed as an S corporation involves more paperwork, why would you choose S corporation tax status? The most common answer is: as a way to reduce self-employment taxes while keeping pass-through taxation. As the owner of an SMLLC classified as an S corporation you are not considered a self-employed individual and are not subject to self-employment tax. Instead, you are considered to be an employee, and—the key point—you can take some, but not necessarily all, available profits from your company as a salary. Other SMLLC profit, if any, can be taken as a dividend, which is not subject to any employment-related taxes, nor—unlike with a C corporation—to double taxation. By contrast, all profit from an SMLLC classified as a disregarded entity is subject to self-employment tax. In short, if your SMLLC is classified as an S corporation for tax purposes, you'll avoid employment taxes on money you receive from the company in the form of a dividend.

Because you pay employment-related taxes on a salary but not on dividends, you might think that you should just take all your money from the SMLLC as a dividend, and thus avoid paying self-employment taxes altogether. This approach, however, is prohibited. The IRS is very clear that you must pay yourself at least "reasonable compensation."

For various reasons, choosing S corporation status strictly to try to save on self-employment taxes can be a questionable proposition. However, if you're seriously considering this approach, you should check with both a lawyer and a tax expert to make sure your SMLLC is properly organized and meets all IRS guidelines, and that reclassification is financially worth your while.

TIP

It can be difficult to know when compensation is reasonable. The IRS website has a list of nine factors to consider in determining the reasonableness of compensation. Court cases also have relied on multiple factors. By way of trying to ensure that compensation will pass muster with the IRS as "reasonable," some accountants apply a 60/40 (or more conservative 70/30) rule, where at least 60% of profit is taken as salary and the rest as a dividend. Unusually low wages as compared to the amount distributed as dividends is a red flag for the IRS. It is also helpful to have comparable salary information for similar businesses using sources like the U.S. Bureau of Labor Statistics or employment agencies.

EXAMPLE: Miranda formed her gourmet catering business ten years ago as an SMLLC. Six years later, she elected to have it taxed as an S corporation. Last year the business did very well and she had a net profit of $100,000. She knows that other people doing the same kind of work normally earn $50,000A–$60,000 per year. She also checked with some government websites and her accountant for additional confirmation that $60,000 is a reasonable salary. She then paid herself a salary for the year of $60,000 (making sure to have her SMLLC deduct employer taxes for Social Security and Medicare, and also making sure to pay her own share of those taxes on her personal tax return). Miranda took the remaining $40,000 as a dividend—and didn't have to pay any employment taxes on that money.

State Income and Franchise Taxes

Along with federal taxes, you'll probably also need to pay state taxes on your SMLLC's income. A few states, like Alaska and New Hampshire, don't have a personal income tax. However, in the vast majority of states, if your SMLLC keeps the default tax classification of disregarded entity, you'll need to pay a state income tax on your SMLLC's profits as part of your personal state tax return. (If you choose to be taxed as a corporation, you'll likely have other requirements, not covered here.)

In addition, some states also have a separate tax that must be paid by all LLCs, including SMLLCs. This tax, sometimes explained as a tax for the privilege of doing business in a particular state, is usually called a franchise tax, a registration fee, or a renewal fee. The way in which it's calculated can vary widely from state to state. In several of the largest states, it's based at least in part on the SMLLC's income. In some other states, it's simply a flat annual fee. For more information about LLC taxes in your state, you can check the websites for your secretary of state and department of revenue (or equivalent state offices). In addition, Nolo has state-specific articles on LLC tax filing requirements in the LLC section of its website.

Employer Taxes

Does your SMLLC have employees? If so, you'll have to pay employer taxes. That's true regardless of how your SMLLC is classified for tax purposes. In most cases, you will need to pay both federal and state employer taxes. That includes paying both withholding tax (which covers each employee's personal income tax) and unemployment insurance (UI) tax. Here's a quick look at each of these two taxes.

Withholding Tax

All employers must withhold a portion of every employee's wages and pay the withheld amount directly to the IRS as partial payment of that employee's federal income tax. In addition, unless your business and employees are located in one of the few states that don't have personal income tax, you also will have to pay state withholding tax.

Basic elements related to federal and state withholding taxes include:

- obtaining a federal Employer Identification Number (EIN) and the equivalent state tax ID number
- making sure you have a federal Form W-4 and equivalent state form on file for each employee
- placing withheld money for taxes in a separate account
- making periodic withholding tax payments
- filing periodic withholding tax returns
- providing W-2s to employees after the end of the year, and
- filing annual withholding tax returns and related information.

Obtain tax ID numbers. You can obtain an EIN (also frequently referred to as an FEIN) by going online at the IRS website. For more details, see Chapter 3. On the state level, most states issue their own, separate tax ID numbers to employers. Just as with an EIN, you usually can apply for the state ID number online. Often you'll need your EIN before you can complete the application for the state-issued number. If at all possible, you should apply for employer ID numbers before you start paying employees.

Have employees complete withholding forms. Employees should complete a federal Form W-4, *Employee's Withholding Allowance Certificate*, before they start working. Employees use Form W-4 primarily to declare allowances (exemptions) that can affect how much tax is withheld.

In addition, most states have a separate state withholding form. Often the name of the form will end in "-4," mirroring the federal "W-4." State withholding forms are used for the same general purpose as the federal form. In fact, a few states simply ask you to use a copy of the federal form. If your state uses a copy of the federal form, you should write or print something on the form to indicate when it's being used for state withholding taxes. In some states, employees may not be required to complete a state form. However, in those cases, employees usually are not entitled to any state withholding allowances.

You should keep the completed forms for your employees on file at your business and update them as necessary. Most forms can be downloaded from the Internet.

Place withheld taxes in a separate account. You should set up a separate account to hold the money you withhold from employee salaries for withholding tax purposes. You will need to make that account available to the IRS and any states where you are required to pay withholding taxes electronically.

Make periodic tax payments. Your federal withholding tax payment schedule will depend on the average amount you withhold from employee wages. The more you withhold, the more frequently you'll need to make withholding tax payments. New employers start on a monthly payment schedule (unless, because of very low withholding, they qualify to pay annually). After you've been an employer for enough time, your schedule will be based on the amount you've withheld in the past (during a so-called lookback period).

Most employers end up with either a monthly or semiweekly schedule for federal payments. Employers with a low annual amount of withholding ($1,000 or less) may only be required to pay once a year. The IRS will specifically inform you if you will be on a payment schedule. In rare cases where an employer withho' amounts of tax, there is a next-day payment requirement.

At the state level, the schedule for making payments varies. Some sta... require payments at the same time you pay your federal withholding taxes. In many states, however, payments are due on a schedule that is different from the federal schedule. Check your state's tax collection agency website for more details.

Many states require employers with larger payrolls (defined differently in different states) to make payments electronically and a few states require all employers to pay electronically. The IRS requires that all withholding tax payments be paid electronically.

File periodic tax returns. You must file quarterly withholding tax returns with the IRS. Use Form 941, *Employer's Quarterly Federal Tax Return*, which you can download from the IRS website. (Businesses with very low annual withholding tax liability—$1,000 or less—may file annually instead of quarterly, using a single Form 944, *Employer's Annual Federal Tax Return*.) Federal returns are due on the last day of the month following the close of the quarter. With limited exceptions, you must file a Form 941 each quarter even if you didn't pay wages during the quarter.

States have their own withholding tax returns. In many cases, the state's taxing agency will send you preprinted returns that already contain some of the information for your business. As with tax payments, many states require at least larger employers to file their periodic returns online. State return due dates may differ from the federal due dates.

Provide W-2s to employees. You must give a federal Form W-2, *Wage and Tax Statement*, to each employee who worked for you during the preceding calendar year. The W-2 summarizes the amounts you withheld for things like Social Security and Medicare for a particular employee. The due date for providing W-2s is January 31 of the year following the year for which you are reporting wages.

File an annual return. You must file copies of the W-2s for all of your employees with the IRS after the end of each calendar year. You transmit those copies using Form W-3, *Transmittal of Wage and Tax Statements.* There are also options for filing electronically. As with W-2s sent to employees, the due date is January 31.

Many states require you to file an annual return and/or annual reconciliation after the end of the calendar year. This is in addition to the periodic returns you file during the course of the year. The filing summarizes your withholding tax information for the preceding year. You generally must include copies of your business's W-2s. In many states, larger employers must make the filing electronically.

TIP

An outside payroll service is often a good idea. Working with employer taxes can be complicated and time-consuming. Depending on your situation, you may want to consider relying on expert assistance like an outside payroll service or payroll software. If you do choose to rely on outside assistance, keep in mind that you, personally, can still be held responsible for any payroll tax mistakes.

Unemployment Insurance Tax

Employers are required to pay federal and state unemployment insurance taxes. Federal unemployment taxes are governed by the Federal Unemployment Tax Act (FUTA). State unemployment taxes are governed by each state's state unemployment tax act (SUTA).

Unlike withholding tax, which doesn't apply at the state level in states that have no personal income tax, a state-level UI tax is assessed in every state. Moreover, unlike withholding tax, employers alone are responsible for paying federal UI tax as well as (in nearly every state) the state UI tax. No money from employee salaries is withheld for UI tax.

Some of the elements relating to withholding tax, such as obtaining a federal EIN and the equivalent state ID number, also apply to UI tax. Additional UI tax requirements include:

- registering with your state's UI tax agency
- determining if your business is liable for UI tax
- determining the UI tax rate for your business
- knowing the UI taxable wage base, and
- filing UI tax reports and payments.

Register your business. In most states, UI taxes are not handled through the standard state taxing authority, such as a department of revenue. Instead, UI taxes usually are handled through a separate state agency devoted to employment. Names vary, but in many states the agency will have a name similar to one of the following:

- Division of Unemployment Insurance
- Department of Labor
- Department of Workforce Development, or
- Division of Employment Security.

In most states you can register online. Once registered, you may be issued a UI tax account number that is separate from your state withholding tax account ID number.

Determine if you're liable. A business generally is liable for federal UI taxes if it meets one of two criteria:

- the business pays wages of $1,500 or more in any calendar quarter, or
- the business has one or more employees for at least some part of a day in any 20 or more different weeks during the calendar year.

Different federal rules apply to domestic (household) employees and agricultural employees (farmworkers).

Most states' UI tax liability rules are the same as, or very similar to, the federal rules. However, there are some exceptions. For example, in California, you are liable for UI taxes once you've paid more than $100 in wages in a calendar year.

CAUTION

Do not misclassify employees as independent contractors.
Employers who use independent contractors rather than hiring employees are
not subject to the UI tax. However, it's important that you do not misclassify an
employee as an independent contractor. This is true as regards both withholding
tax and UI tax. There is a term for this type of misclassification that results in
avoidance of UI taxes: SUTA dumping. If you do misclassify an employee, you
could be subject to penalties and fines.

Determine your tax rate. For many years, the federal UI tax rate has been
6%. State UI tax rates, however, vary widely. Moreover, in some states
the rates are relatively stable while in others they fluctuate every year. In
most states, there is a starting rate that applies to new businesses. That rate
often applies to all types of new businesses except for those involved in the
construction industry (which are subject to a higher rate). However, some
states assign rates depending on each business's "industry" category.

Established employers are subject to a lower or higher rate than new
employers depending on an "experience rating." This means, among other
things, whether a business has ever had any employees who made claims
for state unemployment benefits.

Each year, your state's UI tax agency should send you a tax rate notice
letting you know your rate for the new calendar year.

Know the taxable wage base. You pay UI tax on each employee's wages
up to a maximum annual amount. That amount is known as the taxable
wage base. In recent years, the federal taxable wage base has been $7,000.
At the state level, taxable wage bases vary widely. In some states, the wage
base is not much different than the federal amount. However, in other
states, the wage base is more than twice the federal amount, and in a few
states, the wage base is as high as $40,000.

File reports and payments. You deposit federal unemployment tax money
in an account on a quarterly basis. Payments to the IRS must be made
electronically. You stop depositing FUTA tax once an employee has
reached $7,000 in taxable wages for a calendar year. Payments are due by
the last day of the month following the end of each calendar quarter. In

addition, after the end of the calendar year, you must file IRS Form 940, *Employer's Annual Federal Unemployment (FUTA) Tax Return*. Form 940 provides the IRS with a summary of your unemployment tax payments and other related information.

At the state level, you usually have to file both quarterly payments and quarterly reports. In many states you are required to make payments electronically. As a rule, states require that you file quarterly reports every quarter, regardless of whether you paid wages or owe UI taxes for a quarter. Failure to make full payments or file quarterly reports on time can result in penalties and fines.

One piece of good news is that you usually can credit your state UI tax payments against your federal UI taxes.

> **CAUTION**
> **Having employees isn't just a tax issue.** On the contrary, employees also involve other matters not covered here. As one example, it's illegal to ask certain questions when interviewing potential employees. As another example, you are required to use certain processes (such as e-Verify) and report certain information (often related to child support laws) when hiring employees. And, as a final example, you usually are required to post certain information in conspicuous places for your employees. You can find more information on your obligations as an employer in *The Employer's Legal Handbook*, by Fred S. Steingold, and other Nolo employer-related articles and publications.

Sales and Excise Taxes

You are probably familiar with paying sales tax on goods that you buy. If you are new to running a sales-based business, however, you may be less familiar with sales tax from the seller's perspective. If your SMLLC is engaged in retail sales, you must collect sales tax for each taxable item that you sell and pay those collected taxes to the appropriate state taxing authority.

Sales tax laws, including sales tax rates, are handled on a state-by-state basis. The sales tax you need to charge for a particular item depends on the sales tax rate of the state where the item will be used. If you're located in Iowa and sell to a buyer in Fort Lauderdale, you need to charge Florida's sales tax, and then, as just mentioned, remit that tax money to the state of Florida. If you expand this example to include sales in, say, 25 different states, it quickly becomes clear that it can be cumbersome to deal with sales tax issues. And, of course, making sales in all 50 states (not to mention elsewhere in the world) is a far more likely possibility in the Internet Age, with options like selling on your own website or eBay, and "Fulfillment by Amazon."

TIP
The Streamlined Sales Tax Project (SSTP) works to create more uniform sales tax rules. Most states have participated in the project and approximately half the states have passed legislation that conforms to the SSTP's standards. However, while those standards are intended to make sales taxes more uniform across states, they also pressure out-of-state sellers—such as businesses that sell via the Internet—to collect sales tax even when not otherwise required to do so.

Excise taxes are taxes you have to pay if you:
- make or sell certain products .
- run certain types of businesses
- use various types of equipment, facilities, or products, or
- are paid for certain types of services.

Examples of specific federal excise taxes include taxes on air transportation, taxes related to the use of diesel fuel, gasoline, or kerosene, taxes related to the use of heavy trucks, and taxes on indoor tanning services. In addition, many states have excise taxes for gasoline, alcohol, and cigarettes or other tobacco products.

LLCs Owned by Spouses in Community Property States

From almost every perspective, it's accurate to say that an SMLLC has only one member. After all, that's why it's called a single-member LLC. However, in community property states, you can have an SMLLC with not one but two members—or at least have a two-member LLC that's treated like an SMLLC for tax purposes. Community property states have laws stating that property acquired by a married individual is owned in common with that individual's spouse. These laws can extend to profits from an LLC owned solely by two people married to each other.

The IRS has a special rule applicable to LLCs owned by married couples who live in community property states. Under these special rules, a married couple can treat their jointly owned business as a disregarded entity for federal tax purposes, if:

- their LLC is wholly owned by the spouses as community property under state law
- no one else would be considered an owner for federal tax purposes, and
- the business is not otherwise treated as a corporation under federal law.

In most cases, this would mean that the spouses would file a joint tax return (with the general tax savings that come with such a return), and include with that return a Schedule C, and any other relevant schedules (Schedule SE, Schedule E, and so on), for their business. For all practical (tax) purposes, they would prepare their taxes as though their LLC were an SMLLC. This includes same-sex couples.

If a married couple did not meet the requirements of the IRS special rule, then their jointly owned LLC would be treated like any other multi-member LLC, which means it would be taxed as a partnership, not as a disregarded entity. As a partnership, an LLC has additional tax reporting requirements that don't apply to a disregarded entity, such as filing a partnership tax return.

Forming Your SMLLC: An Overview

n order to form your SMLLC, you'll have to do a bit of research, make a few key decisions, and complete some paperwork. Assuming that you're eligible to form an SMLLC, two of your biggest decisions will be naming your business and deciding how it will be managed. Once you've made those decisions, you'll need to file articles of organization (or an equivalent document) with the state. Most lawyers would also recommend that you prepare an operating agreement for the new company that specifies various rules, rights, and obligations. Next, depending on your company's tax status and whether it has employees, you may also need to obtain a federal employer identification number. And, finally, if your SMLLC will be providing licensed professional services (if you are forming a PLLC), you probably will need to meet certain special requirements.

Can I Form a Single-Member LLC?

Even though LLCs were originally conceived of as companies with multiple members, every state allows you to form an LLC with just one member. However, in most states, certain professions face restrictions or additional requirements regarding the formation of an LLC.

More specifically, if you work in a field such as medicine, law, accounting, architecture, or engineering, in approximately half the states, you won't be allowed to form a standard LLC. Instead, you'll need to form what most states call a professional limited liability company, or PLLC. In most other states, professionals are allowed to form regular LLCs, although these LLCs usually have certain additional requirements and restrictions. Only one state, California, does not permit professionals to form either regular LLCs or PLLCs; if you're in California, your option is to form a professional corporation—or PC—instead. For more information, check the section below on PLLCs.

There are a few types of businesses that are not allowed to form an SMLLC (or any LLC). The most important among these are financial services, which include banks and insurance companies. However, unless you're interested in forming an SMLLC as a subsidiary of a financial services corporation (in which case you'll need assistance outside the scope of this book), this is not likely to be an issue.

Naming Your SMLLC

As part of the process of registering your SMLLC with the state, you'll need to give it a name. Choosing a business name can be fun, but you also have to be careful. You won't be allowed to register a business name that's the same as or very similar to the name of another, preexisting business in your state. To put it in more technical terms, when naming your business it's important not to violate trademark laws. This means avoiding names that might create what in legal jargon is called a "likelihood of confusion" with another business in the same field.

In a pre-Internet age, it was easier for people starting small, local businesses to investigate the uniqueness of the names they wanted to use because it was assumed that there were certain geographic limitations on those names. Nowadays, however, even if your SMLLC name won't conflict with other businesses in your state, you often need to be concerned about trademarks and trade names that may be in use anywhere in the country. If you want to name your Atlanta-based athletic clothing store Jenny's Joggers and there's already a popular online seller based in Anaheim called JennieJoggers, you're probably going to have to find another business name—or else risk a trademark infringement lawsuit. In short, you shouldn't necessarily expect geographic separation to protect you.

The best approach to avoiding trademark issues is to try to make a detailed search of existing business names before settling on a name for your own business. This may include:

- looking at filings for corporations, limited liability companies, and similar entities registered with state and local government offices, such as your secretary of state's office (state-level listings are usually available online)
- a basic Internet search using a search engine such as Google, and
- checking the federal trademark register of the United States Patent and Trademark Office (USPTO) which is available online at www.uspto.gov.

In addition, if you want greater certainty, you can hire a professional service to do a more thorough investigation of the name you are interested in.

TIP

Once you've decided on a business name, reserve it. Almost every state allows you to reserve an LLC name before you actually file papers to legally establish the company. You can reserve a name for 30-180 days depending on the state. In many states, you also can renew the reservation for an additional period. There is almost always a fee to reserve a name. Search the website for your secretary of state (or equivalent state office) for more information.

When choosing your business name, keep in mind that many states require that it contain some indication that the business is an LLC. This is usually accomplished by adding a suffix to the end of the name, such as the letters "LLC" or the words "Limited Liability Company" (for example, Blue River Trail Bikes, LLC). Check your state's LLC laws for the specific rules about naming an LLC in your state.

TIP
You can find more information about names later in this book.
Chapter 6, which covers additional tasks related to running an SMLLC, has a
section with more details about DBAs as well as things like trademarks and
service marks.

Managing Your SMLLC

There are two forms of management for an SMLLC: member-management
and manager-management. In many states, your articles of organization
must indicate whether your SMLLC will be member-managed or manager-
managed. In most states, if you don't designate a management structure
in your formation documents, your LLC will be treated by default as
member-managed. Moreover, some states have specific rules you must
follow to create a manager-managed LLC.

The fundamental difference between the two forms of management
concerns the relationship between ownership and management of your
SMLLC. With a manager-managed SMLLC, you formally create a
role of manager for your SMLLC which is separate from ownership.
With this type of structure, you can appoint someone else or yourself
as manager. In a member-managed SMLLC, the owner is automatically
also the manager.

Under state LLC laws, the manager has the authority to do a wide
range of things on behalf of the LLC, such as entering into contracts,
hiring and firing employees, and taking care of the business's day-to-
day affairs. However, LLC laws generally provide that LLC owners
retain control over certain special or important matters. Typically, these
include things like amending the LLC operating agreement, selling
substantially all of the LLC's assets, dissolving the LLC, or taking any

action outside the ordinary course of the LLC's business. In a manager-managed LLC, the owner's consent normally must be obtained to take these types of actions. Sometimes, however, even these matters can be delegated to a manager by including such authorization in an operating agreement.

TIP

The usefulness of a separate manager role may be more obvious in the context of a multi-member LLC. The owners of most SMLLCs want to be actively involved in managing their companies and, therefore, there is less often the need for a management structure that allows owners to delegate management authority to a nonmember. In contrast, multi-member LLCs may have members who want to be passive investors and not have any management responsibilities. Having the manager-managed LLC option allows you to have a group of passive investors in your membership and to appoint members or non-members to run the LLC's business.

Manager-Managed

To create a manager-managed SMLLC, you must specifically state that you are choosing this type of management structure in your articles of organization. It's also important that you make it clear in your operating agreement that you have a manager-managed SMLLC. As the sole owner and member of the SMLLC, you get to choose who the manager or managers will be. In some situations, you might want to appoint another person as manager and delegate to that person the authority to run the business. For example, if your SMLLC owns rental properties, you might want to delegate to someone else the authority to collect rent, show units to prospective tenants, arrange for repairs, and handle the other day-to-day responsibilities of the business. Or, if your business is large or complex with several different offices or departments, you might choose to have more than one manager.

CAUTION
Be careful about appointing someone else as manager. By default, a manager of a manager-managed SMLLC has a lot of authority. Therefore, when you name a manager, it should be someone you are certain you can trust with your business.

The most common arrangement is for SMLLC owners to name only one manager and to appoint themselves to that role. If you created your SMLLC to run and operate a business on your own, this structure works well: You have sole authority over your SMLLC—both the business operations as manager and the ultimate disposition as the owner. You could choose to delegate certain management authority to others, like authorizing an employee or someone else to write checks on behalf of the business. Or, you could use a power of attorney to give someone else specific, management-like responsibilities, such as selling a parcel of the SMLLC's property. Keep in mind, though, that if you delegate management responsibilities to another person, that person won't be considered a manager in the legal sense of the word. Instead, he or she will only have the specific responsibilities that you have delegated. The overall management authority of the business will remain with you—the manager under state LLC law.

In most cases, there's no problem if you, as owner and sole member, are the only person with the legal authority to run your business. There are, however, two situations where this can become an issue: if you become incapacitated or if you die. To the extent you're concerned about these possibilities, you should have some kind of written provision that appoints someone else as a successor manager to take over as manager if you become incapacitated. Otherwise, if you're the only person with the legal right to make important decisions for your SMLLC and you haven't made any provision for a transfer of management authority, your business could be paralyzed or collapse in your absence.

While planning for these types of serious events is important regardless of whether your SMLLC is member-managed or manager-managed, some legal experts believe it's easier for someone else to take over the running of your business if your SMLLC is manager-managed. Why? Because in a manager-managed SMLLC, the manager role (separate from ownership) is already in place and the authority to delegate management to someone who is not an owner exists by law. By contrast, with a member-managed SMLLC, it's up to you to create and define a management role separate from ownership.

The easiest way to provide for a transfer of management authority is to include a provision in your operating agreement that provides for a successor manager in the event of your incapacity or death (or whatever triggering events you choose). You will want to include the name of the person or clearly identify the person who will be the successor manager. To do this, your operating agreement should include the following:

- that a separate (legal) role of manager exists for your SMLLC (in other words, you have a manager-managed SMLLC)
- who the manager will be in the event of your death or incapacitation or other triggering event, and
- that the person designated as successor manager has authority to act as manager of the SMLLC under state law with any specific limitations or responsibilities that you desire.

If you have any specific issues or concerns with transferring management authority under these circumstances, you should consult with a lawyer.

Depending on your situation, there may be other ways to handle transferring control or ownership of your SMLLC in the event of your incapacity or death. One alternative would be to appoint a family member or trusted friend or employee as an additional manager. That way, if something happened to you, there would be someone else who could immediately step in and take over running the business. However, even prior to something happening to you, the other person would share management authority with you—something you might not want.

There also may be options under trust or estate planning laws that are better suited to your particular needs. Those are more complicated and beyond the scope of this book. If you think you might be interested in something along those lines, you should consult with a lawyer.

Member-Managed

If you don't specify how you want your SMLLC managed in your formation documents, most states will treat your company by default as member-managed. As the owner and sole member of the SMLLC, this means you are also the manager (in the full legal sense of the word). As sole owner/member/manager, you do have the option to delegate certain managerial authority to other people, such as authorizing someone else to write checks for the business or handle the company's bookkeeping. This can be done in your operating agreement or by some other means such as a consent resolution or power of attorney. Delegating certain management responsibilities to another person will not make that other person a manager. That person will only have the specified delegated authority and you—the sole owner—will remain the manager with the general overall authority under state law to run the business. In addition, because you are also the owner, you will not be subject to the limitations on authority that otherwise apply to managers under state law.

With a member-managed SMLLC, options for transfer of full management authority upon the death or incapacitation of the owner/manager include putting a section in the operating agreement, using a separate written resolution, or using other legal documents to transfer control. You may want to consider looking into those options to help ensure your business keeps operating in case something happens to you. As with manager-managed SMLLCs, there also may be options under trust or estate planning laws. Keep in mind that because a member-managed SMLLC does not have a role of manager separate from the owner defined by statute, it may be more complicated or take more time to transfer management authority to another person.

Articles of Organization

There is one document you absolutely must prepare and file in order to form an SMLLC. In most states, that document is known as the articles of organization, and in most states it needs to be filed with the secretary of state. However, your particular state may have a different name for the document (for example, certificate of formation). Or your state may have a different state office where it needs to be filed (for example, in Maryland, the State Department of Assessments and Taxation; in Arizona, the Arizona Corporation Commission).

Different states have different requirements for the articles, but in general each of the following pieces of information must be included:

- the name of your SMLLC
- the name and address of your SMLLC's registered agent
- a statement of the SMLLC's purpose
- an indication of how the SMLLC will be managed
- the address of the SMLLC's principal place of business
- the SMLLC's duration, and
- an authorized signature.

Here's a brief look at each of these items.

Name. As you've already seen, you must make sure that your business's name does not conflict with the name of a preexisting business that's already registered in your state. If you submit articles of organization for an SMLLC named Houdini Linguini, LLC, and there's already a Houdini Linguini, Inc., in your state, your filing will be rejected.

Registered agent. A registered agent is someone that you designate to receive official papers for your SMLLC. These may include renewal notices and other communications from the state—and certainly would include documents related to lawsuits. The registered agent must be located in the state where your SMLLC is organized and you must provide a physical (street) address for the agent. In many cases, you, as owner of your SMLLC, will serve as the registered agent, and the address will be your SMLLC's business location. In other cases, you may choose to appoint a separate party, such as a lawyer or a company, to act as your registered agent.

Statement of purpose. Most states do not require you to be specific about the purpose of your SMLLC. Instead, a statement such as "The purpose of the Limited Liability Company is to engage in any lawful activity for which a Limited Liability Company may be organized in this state" is sufficient. If you want or need a more specific statement, it's usually best to still keep it relatively general, such as "to design, manufacture, and sell clothing and accessories." Also, if you're forming a professional limited liability company (PLLC), you'll need to be more specific about the type of professional services the PLLC will provide (see the section on PLLCs below).

Management. You can choose to structure your SMLLC as either manager-managed or member-managed (see "Managing Your SMLLC," above). States generally require you to indicate which type of management structure will apply for your SMLLC in your articles of organization. In the case of manager-management, you also often need to provide the name and address of each manager in your articles. Under most state laws, if you don't designate a management structure in your formation documents, your LLC will be treated by default as member-managed.

Principal place of business. This is simply the main location for your business. For many SMLLCs, it will be the one and only business location.

Duration. The duration is the length of time, in years, that your SMLLC will operate. Not all states ask that you specify a duration in your articles of organization, and states that do ask for it often do not require you to be specific. Instead, the duration may simply be "perpetual." In fact, in many states, if you do not provide a duration, it's assumed by default to be perpetual. In some states, however, there is a statutory limit on the duration of an LLC. These limits are usually several decades in length, at the end of which time, if the LLC is still in business, the term can be extended for another long period.

Authorized signature. States routinely require at least one organizer of the LLC (or someone authorized to act on their behalf) to sign and date the articles of organization. For an SMLLC, it is frequently the owner (or someone authorized by the owner) who signs the articles.

In addition to the foregoing, there are a few other things to be aware of regarding the articles of organization:

- A small number of states require that you publish your intention to form an SMLLC in a newspaper before you file your articles.
- You may need to prepare your articles differently if you're converting a preexisting business to an SMLLC.
- You'll need to prepare different articles if you're forming a PLLC.

Most state governments have blank forms for the articles of organization that you can download from a website. In many cases, the forms include helpful instructions about how to complete each required item. The forms usually are not specific to single-member LLCs, but instead are for general use with both single- and multi-member LLCs. However, there may be exceptions in a few states, so you should double-check with your secretary of state before filing to make sure you are using the right form.

A large number of states now allow you to file articles of organization online. This usually requires creating a log-in and password on the secretary of state's (or equivalent filing office) website and either responding to a series of questions or completing a blank articles of organization form and submitting it online.

There is almost always a filing fee associated with filing articles of organization. Check your secretary of state's website for current fees.

Once your articles are filed, this will alert people that your business's name is taken (assuming they aren't already on notice because you reserved the name in advance). The articles can also serve as evidence to potential lenders that your business is for real. On a less cheery note, the articles let creditors and others who may have claims against your company know who to contact in order to resolve those claims.

RESOURCE

If you want help creating your SMLLC, check out Nolo's online LLC formation service, which takes care of all the filings, paperwork, and procedural steps necessary to create an SMLLC in any state.

Example Only

Check your secretary of state's website for your state's articles of organization form

---

Articles of Organization

1. Name of Limited Liability Company (must contain the words Limited Liability Company, L.L.C., or LLC, and cannot contain the terms Corporation, Corp., Incorporated, Inc., Ltd., Co., Limited Partnership or L.P.):

   _____

   _____

   _____

2. Name and Address of Registered Agent (must be a street address):

   _____

   _____

   _____

3. Statement of Purpose: _____

   _____

   _____

   _____

4. The Limited Liability Company will be managed by (check one)
   ☐ Members ☐ Managers, whose names and addresses are:

   _____

   _____

   _____

5. Address of Principal Place of Business where records of the company will be kept (must be a street address):_____

   _____

   _____

   _____

Articles of Organization (continued)

6. Duration of the company (perpetual unless otherwise stated):

_____

_____

7. Effective Date for these Articles of Organization: _____

_____

8. Name and Address of Organizer(s): _____

_____

_____

I affirm, under penalties of perjury, having authority to sign hereto, that these Articles of Organization are to the best of my knowledge and belief, true, correct, and complete.

Date _____

Organizer _____

Name _____

Address _____

_____

_____

Organizer _____

Name _____

Address _____

_____

_____

Organizer _____

Name _____

Address _____

_____

_____

The Operating Agreement

An operating agreement lays out the most important rules for how an SMLLC will be run. Unlike the articles of organization, an operating agreement is not required in order to form an SMLLC, nor is it filed with the state. Instead, an operating agreement is optional—though highly recommended.

The importance of an operating agreement may be more obvious in the context of a multi-member LLC. However, an operating agreement also offers important benefits for an SMLLC, such as:

- providing rules that will supersede the default provisions of your state's LLC Act
- serving as an additional document to show potential lenders regarding the organization of your business
- particularly for manager-managed SMLLCs, specifying who will take over management of the business in the event the owner becomes incapacitated or dies
- providing an additional affirmation of the separation of your business from you personally, and
- providing a point of reference for how you originally intended to operate the business.

Most lawyers who form SMLLCs also prepare SMLLC operating agreements for their clients, and many banks and other businesses that you may want to work with will expect you to have this document. You will want to keep this document on file at your business's official location.

 TIP

It's not unusual—or strange—for an SMLLC to have an operating agreement. As the ULLCA says, "It may seem oxymoronic to refer to an 'agreement of ... a sole member,' but this approach is common in LLC statutes." The ULLCA goes on to explain that, "Because LLC statutes make the operating agreement the principal way to override statutory default rules, the advent of single-member LLCs made it necessary to provide that a sole member could make an operating agreement."

Any good operating agreement is tailored to fit the specific needs of the particular SMLLC. For this reason, the length and contents of different companies' operating agreements can vary widely. However, many operating agreements contain information in the following areas:

- organization
- management
- membership
- tax and financial matters
- capital contributions and distributions
- dissolution
- general/miscellaneous provisions, and
- signatures.

This particular list is necessarily somewhat arbitrary; different people (lawyers and others) will include different information, and also will organize the same basic information in different ways. However, an SMLLC operating agreement typically is made between the SMLLC and its sole member (though including the SMLLC as a party to the agreement is not a strict legal requirement); and every properly drafted SMLLC operating agreement will have a section that contains the same basic information as the articles of organization.

Details regarding several of the areas listed above (tax and financial matters, capital contributions and distributions, and dissolution) are covered in other chapters of this book. There are, however, two points worth briefly mentioning here. First, a section on management is particularly important for manager-managed SMLLCs. The section can be used to clearly define the powers, rights, and responsibilities of the manager, as well as how the manager is appointed. It's also one place where, if you, the owner, will serve as the initial manager, you can state who will serve as a successor manager in case you become incapacitated or can no longer act as manager. Second, both a section on management and a section on membership should contain explicit statements of limited liability; in other words, statements that managers and members, respectively, are not liable for debts, obligations, or liabilities of the company.

TIP
There's a sample SMLLC operating agreement at the end of this book. It will give you a clearer idea of what an SMLLC operating agreement can look like. If you want help drafting an operating agreement for your SMLLC, check Nolo's website for its online LLC formation package which includes creating an operating agreement for an SMLLC in any state.

Getting an Employer Identification Number

An employer identification number, or EIN, is a nine-digit number similar to a Social Security number. However, unlike a Social Security number, an EIN is intended for business entities instead of people. Also, while a Social Security number is issued by the Social Security Administration, an EIN—being primarily intended for tax purposes— is issued by the IRS.

Whether your SMLLC is required to have an EIN or not mainly depends on how it's being taxed and whether it has employees. SMLLCs are treated by default as disregarded entities by the IRS and do not file separate income tax returns. Instead, the single member is considered self-employed, and taxes on business income are included as part of the member's personal tax return. If that's your situation, you can use your own Social Security number when filing taxes for the business and you are not required to obtain an EIN.

However, if you choose to have your SMLLC taxed as a corporation, the company is considered a separate entity by the IRS and you are considered an employee of that entity. In that case, your SMLLC will need an EIN. In addition, if your SMLLC has at least one employee (regardless of how your SMLLC is taxed), then you'll need to obtain an EIN. This is because, even if your company is classified as a disregarded entity and you pay taxes on its earnings on your personal tax return, you'll still need an EIN to file the required federal employer taxes with the IRS.

There are other reasons why you might need or want an EIN even if it's not required by tax law. Banks generally require you to have an EIN to open a business account. In addition, companies with which you do business may require an EIN to process payments. And some states require that all LLCs, regardless of federal tax classification, use an EIN on their state tax returns.

Applying for an EIN is a fairly simple process that can be completed online at the IRS website. As long as you have the basic information available in advance, you should be issued an EIN immediately after submitting the online application.

Professional Limited Liability Companies (PLLCs)

A professional limited liability company (PLLC) is a limited liability company owned and operated by one or more licensed professionals. You can form a PLLC with just one member in forty-nine of the fifty states. The only exception is California, which does not allow professionals to form LLCs. In California, single owners who want to organize their business to limit their liability instead must form a professional corporation.

Even though PLLCs are allowed in every state except California, not every kind of professional in every state can form a PLLC. Instead, some states permit members of only certain professions to form PLLCs. Moreover, some states have special laws for forming and operating a PLLC that are separate from the laws for a regular LLC. And, to further complicate matters, regardless of whether a particular state has separate laws for PLLCs, often there are additional requirements for professionals who form an LLC. For example, professionals forming an LLC may have to specify in their articles of organization the professional services to be provided or the members' names. Or they may have to submit professional licensing certifications for their members at the time they file their articles.

In many of the states that don't formally distinguish between PLLCs and regular LLCs, the law simply states that an LLC can be formed for any lawful purpose, which implicitly includes professional services. In those states, professionals usually follow the general rules for forming and operating a regular LLC, subject to any other rules that may apply to professionals in their state.

In sum, because state laws and the rules of professional regulatory boards vary so greatly, it is difficult to generalize about whether and how you might organize your professional practice as a single-member PLLC in your state.

 CAUTION
Check the state laws and professional board rules in your state.
Because there is so much variation in how states handle PLLCs—including many that don't even officially use the term "PLLC"—you should check your state's LLC Act before trying to form a PLLC. Then, you should check for any other laws that may apply, such as a professional entities act or statutes relating to specific professions. Finally, you should look at any rules issued by the regulatory board or agency for your particular profession. Sometimes those rules will impose additional restrictions on forming a PLLC.

While generalizing about PLLCs is difficult, there are several things common to PLLCs in most states. Here's a quick overview.

Not all licensed professionals can form PLLCs. In states with laws that clearly distinguish PLLCs from other LLCs, there usually is a specific list of professions that are allowed to form PLLCs. These lists vary widely from one state to the next. New York, for example, lists more than 30 professions, such as podiatry, acupuncture, massage therapy, and interior design. Some other states have much shorter lists of professions that are permitted or required to form PLLCs. Most states include at least the following professions:

- physicians
- attorneys
- dentists
- accountants
- veterinarians
- architects, and
- engineers.

State licensure required. By definition, you aren't a professional for the purpose of forming a PLLC if you don't have a state-issued license for your profession. You'll need the license before you can set up the PLLC.

Special articles of organization. Some states have a separate articles of organization form specifically for PLLCs. Also, many states require the articles of organization for PLLCs to clearly state that the purpose of the company is to provide a specific type of professional services, which means a more limited statement of purpose than is allowed for non-professional LLCs.

State agency approval. You may need to submit the articles of organization (or equivalent LLC organizational document) to the state regulatory board or agency for your profession or to another state agency, either to get the agency's approval or simply to register your PLLC to provide professional services.

Naming restrictions may apply. Some states don't require that there be any distinction between the names of PLLCs and the names of other LLCs. In those states, all LLCs, including PLLCs, usually are required only to have a suffix such as "LLC" or "Limited Liability Company." However, other states either require or permit PLLC names to end with suffixes such as "PLLC," "PLC," or "Professional Limited Liability Company." Beyond state PLLC laws, professional regulatory boards sometimes have their own additional restrictions on PLLC names.

Membership and service restrictions. Laws for PLLCs often assume there will be multiple members (owners) of the company. With that in mind, laws often state that the owners of a PLLC either all practice the same profession or all practice related professions (such as related health care professions). While this isn't likely to be an issue for a single-member PLLC, it could become relevant if at some point you choose to bring in additional members. Many states also require that PLLCs provide only the professional service (or, possibly, set of related professional services) laid out in the PLLC's articles of organization. In many states, it is also permissible to provide certain directly related, nonprofessional services; sometimes these are referred to as "ancillary" services.

You're still subject to the licensing board. Forming a PLLC can protect you from certain types of liability. However, you still are subject to the rules of the state licensing board for your profession. If you violate any of those rules, you generally can't avoid punishment just because you're operating as a PLLC.

Insurance requirements. You may be required to carry a minimum amount of professional liability (malpractice) insurance. The requirement, including the minimum amount, may vary depending on the profession involved.

You aren't protected from all liability. As with other SMLLCs, if you operate a single-member PLLC, you are protected from being held personally liable for certain things. This includes business debts owed solely by the company. It also includes people who are personally injured in connection with your PLLC because of things having nothing to do with your own professional malpractice or torts (for example, if someone slips and falls in your PLLC's offices). In addition, if at any point you expand the business to include other professionals as co-members, you would not be liable for their malpractice. However, you do remain personally liable if you personally guarantee a loan for the business, if you engage in professional malpractice, or if you intentionally or negligently commit a tort (such as assaulting someone in your office).

Additional Resources

For additional details on forming an SMLLC in your state, check your secretary of state's office (or equivalent office) and state LLC Act. Using the Internet, you should quickly be able to find the office in your state responsible for registering LLCs. Even in states where the office is not called the secretary of state, if you search for the name of your state and "secretary of state" you generally will be directed to the right office. If not, consider adding "llc filings" or a similar term to your search. You can also check www.statelocalgov.net, which allows you to search a state-by-state list of secretary of state offices, as well as search for government offices by state and topic (e.g., Kansas + Secretary of State). If you want to create your SMLLC through an online service that takes care of all the filings, paperwork, and procedural steps necessary to create an SMLLC in any state, check out Nolo's online LLC formation package.

To find your state's LLC Act, you should be able to run a similar online search using your state's name and "llc act." You can also check www.nolo.com for state specific articles related to SMLLCs and LLCs—in some cases, those articles will contain links to the relevant statutes. Be aware that some states make their laws more easily available, or more readable, than others. In some cases, you may be directed to a state legislature website that will require additional navigation (and patience) before you reach the text you're looking for. In other cases, you will be redirected to a site operated by a private company, such as Lexis, and, again, will need to do a bit of further navigating in order to see the LLC Act.

It's very possible that you'll be able to properly set up your SMLLC without the help of a lawyer. However, if, after doing your own research and using Nolo's resources and services (including this book), you still have questions, working with a lawyer may be worth your while. When trying to find a good lawyer, consider checking with other small business owners in your area, particularly those with businesses similar to yours. Another possible source for lawyer recommendations is professionals you work with in connection with your own business, such as bankers, accountants, or real estate agents. Finally, websites and Internet listings may be of some use—but when using these sources, you should investigate the backgrounds of any lawyers you're considering, including their education, years of experience, and areas of specialization (such as small business law). The Nolo website (www.nolo.com) has a lawyer directory which includes lawyers by practice area and location.

Financing, Conversion, and Dissolution

This chapter covers several diverse matters. The first two sections deal with how capital (money and other assets) gets paid into your SMLLC and how you get money and, potentially, other capital back out of the business. Next, there's a section on how to convert to an SMLLC from another form of business. The final section provides an overview on how to dissolve or close down your SMLLC.

Capital Contributions and Capital Interest

When establishing a new SMLLC, you'll want to provide some kind of initial investment in the business. This type of pay-in is technically known as a capital contribution. Most often, a capital contribution will be in the form of cash—for example, you invest $5,000 of your personal savings in the new SMLLC. However, LLC laws allow for several different kinds of capital contributions, including:

- money
- property
- services, or
- a promise to contribute money, property, or services in the future.

Whatever you contribute—money, property, or services—becomes the property of the SMLLC.

An initial capital contribution is commonly seen as being given in exchange for membership in an LLC. However, while not typical, a person could contribute something to a company without being given membership, and a person could also be given membership without making any contribution.

! CAUTION
Making an initial contribution is strongly recommended. While most people do make an initial capital contribution, legally it is not required. You could simply appoint yourself as the sole member of your SMLLC without making any initial investment. However, you'd probably be taking a significant risk if you didn't invest at least a small amount at the outset. Without any capitalization, your business may not appear to be truly separate from you, personally. In other words, without any initial contribution, if your business is responsible for someone being injured, or incurs a debt that it's unable to pay, a court might hold that your company suffered from inadequate capitalization. It therefore might allow someone with a claim against your business to "pierce the veil" of limited liability associated with your SMLLC, and go after you, personally, for restitution.

Making a money contribution can be very simple: You write a check from your personal account and deposit it in your new business account. Moreover, you don't necessarily have to invest a large amount—for some very small businesses, a few hundred dollars might be plenty. The main point is to pay in enough money to meet your initial expenses. Then, going forward, it's important always to keep enough capital in your business to meet your reasonable, ongoing expenses. (This last point is generally a requirement under states' LLC laws.)

Making a contribution in the form of property or services can be somewhat more complicated. The complications mainly relate to potential tax consequences. In most cases, a key issue will be determining the dollar value of the property or services contributed.

For example, if you contribute a piece of real estate you already own that is worth more than when you first acquired it, you'll need to know how much the value increased before you contributed it to your new company. Then, if you ever sell your membership—in effect, sell your company—you'll have to pay taxes on that amount of increased value. Similar tax issues arise relating to property value if you take profits from your company within two years of the date that you contribute the property. Briefly, the IRS may view the taking of profits in such cases as a disguised sale of the property. For further guidance on this point, you should consult with a tax professional.

> **EXAMPLE:** Five years ago, Rudy bought a very small office building for $30,000. It is now worth $50,000. When he forms his new SMLLC, Rudy transfers ownership of the office to the company as a capital contribution. Rudy makes sure to record that the value of the property increased by $20,000 between the time he bought it and the time he contributed it to the SMLLC. In addition, if Rudy wants to take money out of the company to pay himself during the next two years, he'll speak with a tax expert to make sure there won't be any problems with the IRS thinking he actually was trying to sell the property rather than contribute it.

If you intend to contribute services in exchange for your membership (sometimes called "sweat equity"), you'll need to record the value of those services on your company's balance sheet. In turn, you'll need to pay taxes on the value of those services, just as if you'd been paid for them as an employee. (Employee tax issues are covered in Chapter 2.) The value you give to contributed services should be their fair market value. In other words, they should be equal to the typical, reasonable amount you would be paid for those services if you provided them to a typical customer or client.

EXAMPLE: Laura's new SMLLC is a part-time furniture building and restoration business. Laura wants to make an initial contribution to the company in the form of services. More specifically, she is going to build furniture for her SMLLC's office and create several permanent fixtures for her SMLLC's showroom. Laura normally charges customers $100 per hour for these services—this is the fair market value of her services on an hourly basis. She spends 80 hours building furniture and fixtures for the SMLLC. Therefore, in her business's financial records, she can record a contribution valued at $8,000.

For any LLC, an initial contribution usually is exchanged for some portion of ownership in the new company. This ownership portion is called a capital interest. A member's capital interest generally is equal to the percentage of the company he or she owns. While figuring out this percentage can sometimes be complicated in the case of multi-member LLCs, in the case of an SMLLC the matter is straightforward: The single member has a 100% capital interest in the company.

Distributions

Taking money from your company to pay yourself is technically known as a distribution. Depending on a variety of details, such as whether your SMLLC is taxed in the usual manner (as a so-called disregarded entity) as opposed to some special way (for example, as a corporation), a distribution can take various forms. In the typical case, you would simply write yourself a check from your business's operating account as and when needed—but always making sure not to take more money from the company than it needs to meet its financial obligations. (As covered in more detail in the chapter on taxation, if your SMLLC is taxed as a disregarded entity, you'll be taxed on 100% of your company's annual profits each year regardless of whether you take any of those profits for yourself.)

If you do choose to have your company taxed as a corporation—which is an unusual choice for most SMLLCs—you'll have the option to distribute profits to yourself in the form of dividends, salary, or officer compensation. A dividend is subject to double taxation (both the company and you, personally, are taxed); a salary, however, is taxed only once. Consequently, paying yourself a salary is usually the preferred approach. Also, keep in mind that there is additional paperwork if you are dealing with paying yourself from an SMLLC taxed as a corporation. (Again, these matters are covered in more detail in the taxation chapter.)

If you want further guidance on handling distributions, there are several full-length Nolo business books you can check, such as *Form Your Own Limited Liability Company* and *Your Limited Liability Company: An Operating Manual,* both by Anthony Mancuso. In cases where you also have employees who are receiving wages, you may want to consult with an accountant.

CAUTION

Keep good records of all payments. In all cases, including the typical case where you simply write a check from your business account to pay yourself, it's important to keep clear records. Always make sure to document all payment transactions, including payments to yourself.

Converting a Preexisting Business to an SMLLC

Many people who form an SMLLC already have a business and simply want to change that business's legal form. In most cases, the preexisting business is a sole proprietorship. However, other possibilities also exist, such as where a partnership ends and one of the partners chooses to continue the business on his or her own, or a one-person business originally organized as a corporation is converted to an SMLLC.

Converting From a Sole Proprietorship

Just as with forming a new business as an SMLLC, converting a sole proprietorship to an SMLLC primarily involves preparing two key documents: the articles of organization and the operating agreement. As covered in the previous chapter, your articles of organization get filed with the secretary of state, and you keep your operating agreement at your place of business. Keep in mind that some states have a different name for the articles of organization. Also, the operating agreement, while highly recommended, is not strictly required.

After you've filed your articles of organization and prepared your operating agreement, your sole proprietorship's assets and liabilities generally will transfer directly to your new SMLLC without your needing to take any further steps. If your sole proprietorship had a single bank account with $10,000 in it, after the conversion that amount will be the property of your new SMLLC. Similarly, if your sole proprietorship had unpaid bills totaling $3,000, those debts will now be owed by the new company. If, however, your sole proprietorship had a loan, for example from a bank, you'll have to contact the lender to determine how—or if—that loan can be transferred to your newly formed SMLLC.

There also are special rules regarding whether a sole proprietorship converting to an SMLLC needs a new employer identification number (EIN). In most cases, there are two points you'll need to pay attention to. First, if you've never had an EIN, or only had one under your own name, you'll need a new EIN for your SMLLC if:

- you're paying wages to employees, or
- you're paying excise taxes.

Second, you'll also need to obtain an EIN if you choose to have your new SMLLC taxed as a corporation or an S corporation. (There are some additional details about EINs in the chapter on taxation.)

Converting From a Partnership

If you're ending a partnership and now going it alone, then, just as with converting from a sole proprietorship, you'll need to file articles of organization and prepare and keep an operating agreement. However, unlike converting from a sole proprietorship, before you file to form an SMLLC, you first need to properly close down—or, in legal lingo, dissolve and wind up—your partnership. When dissolving and winding up, you'll want to make sure that each of your soon-to-be-former partners receives his or her full share of the partnership's assets, and also that all debts, liabilities, and claims are properly assigned or resolved. This last point is particularly important: You want to make sure that down the road, after you're running an SMLLC and ostensibly covered by limited liability, you aren't unexpectedly hit with a lawsuit or claim for money against you personally because the matter somehow was left over from the partnership. With that in mind, you should strongly consider working with a lawyer to make sure you fully and properly dissolve your preexisting partnership before establishing your SMLLC.

One other point to keep in mind when moving from a partnership to an SMLLC is that you'll handle your taxes slightly differently. In both cases, the business itself doesn't pay taxes, and instead all tax liability passes through directly to you (so-called pass-through taxation). However, where a partnership needs to file a partnership tax return (IRS Form 1065), an SMLLC filing as a sole proprietorship uses IRS Schedule C attached to the single member's personal federal tax return. Also, as part of winding up, you'll need to make sure all taxes owed by the partnership are properly paid; because a partnership involves more than one person, and an SMLLC has just one owner, generally you can't simply carry over tax obligations to the new company.

Converting From a Corporation

It's rare for a small business to be established as a one-person corporation and then convert to an SMLLC. However, if this is the situation you're facing, you'll have a much more complicated conversion process. The exact details will depend on the state where your business is incorporated. The potential good news is that, in recent years, quite a few states have moved to a (relatively) simplified conversion process.

CAUTION
Even where the simplified corporation conversion process is available, you won't be able to avoid owing taxes when converting your corporation to an SMLLC. The details are too complicated to cover here, but, in general terms, the IRS will treat the conversion of your corporation as a sale of your business, and you'll owe taxes on that sale. If you're looking at converting a corporation to an SMLLC, you definitely should get assistance from a tax professional to learn what kind of tax bill you'd be looking at, and what paperwork you'd need to complete in order to pay it.

In general, there are three methods for converting a corporation into an SMLLC. In many states, the new, simplified process, called statutory conversion, is available. With a statutory conversion, you, as the one shareholder and only director of the corporation, approve the conversion and file a certificate of conversion—and, as necessary, an LLC certificate of formation or other documents—with the secretary of state. Tax consequences aside, your corporation's assets and liabilities are automatically transferred to your new SMLLC.

In most other states, your best available option will be a statutory merger. With a statutory merger, you begin by forming your new SMLLC. At that point, when there's both the preexisting corporation and the newly created SMLLC, you approve a merger of the two entities. Next, you formally exchange your corporation shares for your SMLLC membership (this usually involves a written merger agreement). Finally, you'll likely also have to file a form with the secretary of state that formally dissolves your corporation. As with statutory conversion, your corporation's assets and liabilities are automatically transferred to your SMLLC.

In a few states, your only option will be a nonstatutory conversion. Like a statutory merger, you'll need to begin by forming your new SMLLC. Then you'll need to formally transfer corporation assets and liabilities to that new company, as well as formally exchange your corporation shares for SMLLC membership. Once that's done, you'll need to formally dissolve and liquidate the corporation. If you have to undertake a nonstatutory merger, you definitely should seek expert legal assistance.

You can find more details for your state in the Business Formation section of Nolo's website (see the Dissolving an LLC section for articles on converting LLCs).

CAUTION

Conversions involve more tasks than are covered here. Even in the simplest case of converting a sole proprietorship to an SMLLC, taking care of the articles of organization and operating agreement isn't the end of the process. Apart from possibly needing to obtain an EIN as discussed above, you'll also need to update the name on all relevant business documents. This includes things like bank accounts, insurance policies, licenses and permits, titles to vehicles or other important personal property, and any documents, including titles, relating to real estate owned by the business. Beyond that, you should also make sure to inform customers, clients, vendors, and others that deal with your business of the change.

Dissolving and Winding Up Your SMLLC

While this book is mainly concerned with starting and running an SMLLC, the following sections briefly cover the process of closing down—or dissolving and winding up—the business.

Dissolution

Your first step is to look at your company's formational documents—the articles of organization and operating agreement. In some cases, one of those two documents will contain a section with rules for dissolution. If, however, neither your articles of organization nor operating agreement has any such rules, most states will allow you to approve dissolution by simply recording that you, as the sole SMLLC member, want to dissolve the company. Regardless of whether you are following rules in a formational document or your state's LLC statute, you should make sure to record your decision in writing.

In most states, after deciding to dissolve your SMLLC, you must file articles of dissolution with the secretary of state. In some states, you need to file articles of dissolution or a separate document before you begin winding things up; in others, the filing comes later. Different states require that different information be included in the articles of dissolution, but commonly required items include:

- the name of the SMLLC
- the reason for filing the articles of dissolution (such as your vote or consent), and
- the effective date of dissolution if other than the filing date.

In most cases, you should be able to find an articles of dissolution form and instructions on how to file on your secretary of state's website. The fee for filing the articles of dissolution also should be listed on the website. Be aware that your business name will become available for use by others after you file for dissolution.

CAUTION

You may need to obtain tax clearance when you dissolve the business. Apart from filing articles of dissolution, some states require that you receive some form of clearance or approval from the department or agency that's responsible for collecting taxes (such as a department of revenue). In other cases, clearance may not be necessary, but you will be urged or required to inform the department or agency of the dissolution after it has been processed by the secretary of state. You may also need to close out a state business tax account. You should check the website for the relevant state department or agency for details. In addition, some states will require you to notify the attorney general that you're closing your business. As with tax clearance, you should check the appropriate state website for details.

Winding Up

Following the formal decision to dissolve, your SMLLC continues to exist for the purpose of taking care of certain final matters that, collectively, are known as winding up the company. Under typical LLC laws, key winding up tasks include:

- continuing company activities and preserving company property for a reasonable time
- prosecuting and defending lawsuits
- ultimately disposing of and transferring the company's property
- discharging the company's debts, obligations, or other liabilities, and
- distributing to yourself any remaining company assets.

Regarding the last two listed items, discharging liabilities and distributing remaining assets, you're generally required to make payments in a particular order. First, you must pay, or make adequate provision to pay, creditors. (It is particularly important that you pay all outstanding taxes.) Then, after those debts and any other liabilities are taken care of, you can distribute remaining assets to yourself.

One other key task is giving notice of your SMLLC's dissolution to creditors and other claimants. In most cases, giving notice is optional. However, doing so will help limit your liability and also make it safer for you to take for yourself any remaining assets. Laws vary by state, but in most cases, one way to give notice is by sending a written document directly to known claimants after dissolution. Generally, the written notice must:

- describe the information that must be included in a claim
- provide a mailing address where a claim may be sent
- state the deadline for bringing the claim (generally there is a minimum length of time for this deadline, such as 120 days after sending the notice or filing of articles of dissolution), and
- state that the claim will be barred if not received by the deadline.

In most states, you can also give notice to unknown (potential) claimants by publishing in a newspaper. As with sending direct notice to individual claimants, there usually are specific rules for giving notice through publication. In many states, claimants have three years after the date of newspaper publication to bring a claim; however, the length of time can vary between two years and five years depending on the state.

Canceling Registrations in Other States

Finally, if your LLC is registered or qualified to do business in other states, you must file separate forms to terminate your right to conduct business in those states. Depending on the states involved, the form might be called a termination of registration, certificate of termination of existence, application of withdrawal, or certificate of surrender of right to transact business. Failure to file the additional termination forms means you'll continue to be liable for annual report fees and minimum business taxes.

Liability Concerns for SMLLCs

By default, all LLCs, including SMLLCs, are assumed to be separate entities from their members. Because of this assumed separateness, LLCs as a rule do not share liability with their members. Among other things, this means that if an LLC has unpaid debts or harms people, it normally is the LLC alone that is held legally responsible. (This is what is meant by limited liability and—as mentioned throughout this book—limited liability is a key reason why small business owners often choose to form LLCs.)

At the same time, the general rule that LLCs are separate from, and don't share liability with, their members also usually means that if an LLC member has unpaid personal debts, a creditor can't collect payment by taking control of the LLC and selling off its assets.

However, there are situations where the normal LLC rules don't apply. The veil that protects LLC members from the LLC's liability can be pierced (set aside) if a court decides that the LLC isn't truly a separate entity from its members. For reasons discussed below, this is potentially more likely with an SMLLC than with a multi-member LLC. In addition, because an SMLLC has just one member, the general rule blocking personal creditors from taking full control of an LLC also can be less likely to apply. In this chapter, we look at both of these potential situations.

CAUTION

The rules relating to the relationship between LLC liability and personal liability historically are concerned with multi-member LLCs. Liability laws specifically for SMLLCs are relatively new and still evolving. If this is an issue of particular concern, be sure to check your state's laws for the latest rules on SMLLCs and protection from personal creditors. Each of the sections in this chapter begins by discussing LLCs generally and then, as appropriate, covers issues specific to SMLLCs.

> ⚠ CAUTION
> **You are not shielded from every kind of liability related to your SMLLC.** For example, you are personally liable if you personally guarantee a loan for your business. Similarly, you can be held personally liable for your own careless behavior if you injure someone while operating your business. And if you're a professional, you can be held personally liable for your own malpractice. However, the latter exceptions aside, your SMLLC should provide you with personal protection from most kinds of business liability.

Piercing the Limited Liability Company Veil

In certain cases, an LLC may be sued and a court may enter a judgment against the company. Key instances where this might happen include the LLC not paying business debts or the LLC being responsible for physical harm to customers or clients. Courts generally take limited liability very seriously in these situations. If the LLC is not able to satisfy the judgment (which usually means paying money), courts typically will not allow the injured party to pierce the limited liability company veil and go directly after an LLC member.

However, under certain conditions, courts will set aside limited liability. In those rare cases, a person with a money judgment against an LLC could, for example, go after an LLC member's personal bank accounts, personal investment accounts, and home.

The exact conditions necessary to allow a plaintiff to pierce the LLC veil vary from state to state. However, in general terms, two factors must be present.

First, there must be a unity of interest between the LLC and its members. In other words, the injured party must show that the LLC is not really a separate entity from its members. The legal system has special phrases for this situation, such as that the business is a mere alter ego of its owners, or is a mere instrumentality of its owners.

Second, the injured party must show that piercing the limited liability veil is necessary to avoid either the perpetration of a fraud or an injustice. This usually means showing that the LLC owner or owners were intentionally using the company to lie to someone or otherwise harm someone.

It's important to understand that both factors—unity of interest and fraud or injustice—need to be present in order for LLC members to lose limited liability protection. Unity of interest, alone, without fraud or injustice, generally would not allow someone with a judgment against an LLC to gain access to a member's personal assets.

It's also important to understand that an owner choosing to organize a business as an LLC in order to gain protection from personal liability, by itself, is not a reason for a court to pierce the limited liability company veil. On the contrary, the general desire of a business owner to gain this protection—so long as it's not abused—is a primary reason why LLCs exist as a business form.

CAUTION

The requirements for piercing the LLC veil are taken from older law relating to liability of corporations. Corporation law predates the widespread adoption of the LLC form. Because corporations have important differences from LLCs—for example, corporations have more required formalities—the rules for corporations are not always easily transferred to LLCs. Courts in some states have recognized this fact and tried to make adjustments in their rules for how to decide LLC veil-piercing cases.

Distinguishing Yourself From the Business

Courts generally look at multiple factors when trying to determine unity of interest (lack of separation or distinction between your SMLLC and you). The specifics vary by state, with some jurisdictions citing a dozen or more factors. In general, no single factor is necessarily decisive, and how a court weighs each factor will vary from one case to the next.

The most common relevant factors are:

- undercapitalization of the business
- commingling of business and personal funds
- failure to clearly assume obligations in the name of the LLC
- failure to communicate with others in the name of the LLC
- failure to follow LLC formalities, and
- small size of the LLC.

Here's a brief look at each of these factors.

Undercapitalization. When you first form your SMLLC you should make an adequate initial investment in the new business. This initial capitalization may not need to be very large—what is an appropriate amount will depend on your specific business. A manufacturing business with a lot of machinery, inventory, factory space, and employees likely would have larger initial expenses, and therefore need a larger initial investment, than a one-person bookkeeping service. You should also make sure that you keep enough money in your SMLLC's bank account on an ongoing basis to cover reasonable upcoming expenses. Adequate ongoing capitalization usually is a legal requirement. If you do not form your SMLLC with an adequate (or any) initial investment, or do not maintain adequate (or any) assets on a continuing basis, your business will run a serious risk of appearing to be a mere empty shell without any financial substance, and a court therefore may find you aren't entitled to limited liability protection.

TIP

You aren't required to keep enough money in your business to cover very unusual or unexpected expenses. For example, you aren't required to keep an extra million dollars in your business account just in case the business gets hit with a huge personal injury lawsuit. (However, for many businesses, it's a very good idea to have liability insurance.)

Commingling of funds. Your SMLLC should have its own bank account. Payments your business receives for its goods and services should be deposited in that account, and money in the account should be used only for business purposes. (Paying yourself a salary is a legitimate business purpose and does not constitute commingling of funds.) Money in your business account should not be used to pay for any personal expenses. Similarly, you should avoid using your personal bank account to pay for any business expenses. If you routinely use your SMLLC account to pay personal expenses, routinely deposit business payments in your personal account, or routinely use personal funds to pay for business expenses, you will blur the distinction between your SMLLC and yourself. In the event of a lawsuit against your SMLLC, this blurring could make it more likely that a court would find that your SMLLC was not a separate entity from you.

Failure to clearly assume obligations in the name of the SMLLC. Whenever you enter into contracts for your SMLLC, you should make clear that you are acting as a representative of the business. In practical terms, this means that when you sign a contract for your SMLLC, for example in relation to getting a loan, you should make sure the name of your SMLLC (e.g., "Apogee Services, LLC") appears prominently above your signature or under the signature line so it's clear that the LLC—and not you personally—is the party to the contract. Equally important, you should make sure that under your signature where your name is printed, you include a title like "Member" or "President" next to your name to show you are signing on behalf of the SMLLC. Otherwise, if you sign a promissory note for a loan to your SMLLC but do not include any mention of the LLC or your title with your signature, you might leave yourself open to personal liability if your business is unable to repay the loan.

Failure to communicate in the name of the SMLLC. Similar to the previous item, all communications for your business should state your SMLLC's name. For your emails, use the name of your SMLLC in your signature block. For voicemail greetings, it is a good idea to mention "LLC." For bills and letters you send out, use the name of your SMLLC in your letterhead. For directory listings and advertising, show the name of your business including "LLC."

Failure to follow formalities. One of the advantages of an LLC over a corporation is that it gives an owner essentially the same limited liability protection but without requiring the same amount of formalities. For example, unlike corporations, LLCs are not required to hold annual meetings or keep written records of important decisions. Consequently, a failure to hold regular member meetings or keep written resolutions of decisions may be less important than other factors to a court trying to decide if an SMLLC is truly separate from its owner. Of course, in the case of an SMLLC, with only one member, it may be questionable what a "meeting" would consist of, and also may be somewhat questionable why a sole owner would need to document decisions in writing. However, if you want to take the safest approach, you should keep written records of important decisions. It's also important to note that, while not necessarily emphasizing SMLLC meetings or resolutions, courts have taken into account an SMLLC's lack of financial and tax records in some piercing cases. (You can find more information about tax and other records in the chapter on record keeping.)

CAUTION
The default rules for LLC formalities can be overridden by an operating agreement. If your operating agreement includes provisions for holding meetings, documenting decisions, or any other formalities, you should make sure to strictly follow those provisions. Failure to do so could be seen by a court as evidence that you weren't taking seriously the idea that your SMLLC is separate from yourself.

An SMLLC at Work

Here's an example of how a small side business or hobby might grow and evolve into an SMLLC. Note the important steps the business owner takes along the way to ensure she gets the liability protection she seeks in creating an SMLLC for her business.

The Story of Belinda Bakes, LLC

For years, Belinda has earned blue ribbons for her baking. Now Belinda also wants her baking to earn some money. She has just set up a bakery and catering service that will operate out of a small storefront. She has formed the new business as an SMLLC: Belinda Bakes, LLC. Along with filing articles of organization with the state, she has also worked with an attorney to prepare an operating agreement.

After the documents were finalized, she opened up a business bank account, providing copies of the necessary documents to the bank. In opening the account, Belinda made an initial deposit of $10,000—this matches the amount mentioned in her operating agreement as her initial capitalization. Going forward, as bills come in for things like baking ingredients, pots, pans, and bowls, electric mixers and gas ovens, rent, utilities, and insurance, as well as monthly payments for a loan she'll later need, Belinda always makes sure she keeps enough money in the business account to cover these types of expenses. She'll also make sure to use this account exclusively for business purposes, paying only business (not personal) expenses from the account and depositing only business (not personal) income into the account. Belinda has a personal bank account, too, but she won't use that for her business. When Belinda rents the storefront, she signs the lease under the printed business name "Belinda Bakes, LLC," and after her signature she prints her name and includes the word "Member" after it. She'll sign the same way when she gets a loan to expand the business. Eventually Belinda may

An SMLLC at Work (continued)

use an assumed name for her bakery, but for now in her advertisements in a local magazine and on her website, she always uses "Belinda Bakes, LLC" as her business name. Similarly, at the end of all her emails and on the bakery's voicemail, her business is called "Belinda Bakes, LLC." This makes it clear that, even if Belinda herself is doing the baking, her operation is organized as a limited liability company.

Because Belinda's attorney suggested it would be a good idea to put into the operating agreement that the LLC will document big decisions—like expanding to a second location—Belinda makes sure to do just that, creating a written resolution when it comes time to rent a second storefront. Of course, Belinda will also keep records of all the bills she receives and all the sales she makes, as well as keeping copies of her tax returns for the required period of time. By doing all these things, Belinda will help ensure that, if anything ever goes horribly wrong—for example, if Belinda Bakes, LLC, is deeply in debt and can't pay its rent or bills, or a Belinda Bakes, LLC, customer is injured by eating something from the bakery—Belinda herself will be protected from personal liability.

Small size of LLC. There is some evidence that suggests that courts are more likely to find that closely held companies are not separate from their owners. (A closely held company is one with few owners.) For example, some courts give weight to whether just one or a few people have "pervasive control" of an LLC. This is partly because a company with fewer owners can more easily plot or scheme to abuse the LLC form for purposes of fraud or other injustice. Clearly the smallest possible LLC is a single-member LLC. It is particularly easy for a single, unscrupulous person to create an SMLLC and then use it improperly or illegally. While there isn't much you can do about greater judicial scrutiny of SMLLCs (assuming it exists), a few legal commentators suggest there is a greater risk in creating an LLC with just one member.

Fraud or Injustice

Here's a brief explanation of what might be involved in committing fraud or creating an injustice such that a court might set aside an LLC's limited liability. In most cases, this involves LLC owners intentionally using an LLC to get money under false pretenses or otherwise unfairly take advantage of other people or entities. This might mean an owner from the start created an SMLLC simply to try to get money from others and without the SMLLC ever engaging in legitimate business activities. It also might mean that an owner of a preexisting SMLLC would remove all the money from the SMLLC's bank account in order to avoid having to pay a legitimate business debt or court judgment. Recently, a federal judge deciding an Illinois case stated that whether LLC separateness would promote injustice "is best understood as asking whether there has been an abuse of limited liability, as when the owner of a party [an LLC] to a contract strips the party [the LLC] of assets so that if it breaks the contract the other party [such as a bank or other creditor] will have no remedy."

> **EXAMPLE:** Jack, an unscrupulous person, files the necessary paperwork to form an SMLLC but invests no money in the new company. Jack then manages to get a $50,000 loan, supposedly for the SMLLC, by stating to the lender that the SMLLC has assets worth more than $100,000. However, Jack in fact uses the loan money entirely for personal purposes, including taking vacations, buying a new sports car, and gambling at a casino. Jack never pays back any of the loan and the lender eventually files a lawsuit for repayment. In the course of the legal action, it becomes clear that Jack never put any of his own money into the SMLLC, never kept any SMLLC financial records, and operated the SMLLC out of his car. It also becomes clear that the SMLLC never received any money except for the loan and never paid any taxes. At one point, under questioning, Jack admits that he intended to use the SMLLC only as a means to get money for personal use. Under these circumstances, it is quite possible that Jack would not be entitled to limited liability protection, and the lender could try to get its money back from Jack's personal assets.

One interesting point about this example is that whether Jack loses limited liability protection might ultimately depend on what the lender knew, or should have known, before making the loan. More specifically, if a court found that the lender knew or should have known that Jack's SMLLC in fact had no assets, then, in spite of Jack's unscrupulous behavior, the court might find that Jack is still entitled to limited liability protection.

Are SMLLC Assets Protected From Personal Creditors?

Members of LLCs, including SMLLCs, may have personal debts for which the LLC is not responsible. For example, an LLC member might rack up $25,000 in charges on a personal credit card for nonbusiness items, such as clothes or kitchen appliances, or receive a $50,000 home equity loan from a bank to remodel bedrooms and bathrooms. If the member is unwilling or unable to repay these types of legitimate personal debts, the person or entity that lent the money (the creditor) generally has the option to go to court to force the member (the debtor) to pay.

In all states, personal creditors not only can go after a debtor's personal assets, such as garnishing wages from paychecks, but also, to one degree or another, can gain rights relating to a debtor's LLC memberships. The exact LLC membership rights that a creditor may obtain vary from state to state. However, generally speaking, personal creditors may have up to three options regarding LLC memberships and assets:

- a charging order
- foreclosure, and
- dissolution.

These three options are listed in ascending order of potential control over an LLC member's interests in the company, with charging orders giving the least control.

All states allow charging orders. However:

- about a dozen states limit creditors to charging orders only and explicitly do not permit foreclosure

- conversely, roughly a third of the states explicitly allow foreclosure, and
- statutes in roughly another third of the states are silent on the issue of whether foreclosure is an option.

Both among states that permit only charging orders and those that allow foreclosures, there are a small number of states where the laws indicate that these are not the exclusive options available to creditors. Those other options, not covered here, could be based, for example, on legal concepts known as fraudulent transfer and reverse veil piercing. In recent years, some states have revised their creditor laws in this area and a few have included provisions that relate specifically to SMLLCs (these are mentioned below).

TIP

If you're particularly concerned about protecting your SMLLC assets, take a close look at your state's rules for creditors. There should be a section of your state's LLC act that covers the issue. You can also check Nolo's website for information on SMLLC asset protection, including state specific articles on the subject.

Charging Orders

A charging order is a court order relating to money from the LLC that would be paid to a member as a distribution. An LLC member generally earns money from an LLC by receiving distributions of profits. A charging order places a lien on those distributions, making them payable to the creditor rather than to the member.

A charging order, however, is useful to a creditor only if the LLC actually makes distributions. If the LLC does not make distributions to the indebted member, a creditor who has a charging order but no additional orders or rights, will not get any money or assets from the LLC.

All states allow creditors to obtain charging orders for LLC membership interests. In addition, LLC laws in about a dozen states limit creditors to charging orders and explicitly do not permit foreclosures. The most common reason given for limiting creditors in this way is that it would be unfair to other members of a multi-member LLC to be forced to share management and control of their LLC with an outsider/creditor for debts that are unrelated to the LLC or its business.

However, this rationale for limiting creditors to charging orders does not carry over to SMLLCs. Because an SMLLC has only one member, no other LLC members (other than the debtor) can be harmed if a creditor is allowed to share in the management or control of the business. With this in mind, and as the number of SMLLCs continues to grow, some state legislatures and courts have made a distinction between creditors' rights regarding multi-member LLCs and SMLLCs, and have expanded creditors' rights when the debtor is the owner of an SMLLC. More specifically, two states that otherwise limit creditors to charging orders—Florida and New Hampshire—have statutes that allow creditors to go further when suing owners of SMLLCs. Under the laws in these states, creditors of SMLLCs (under certain conditions) can take over all the SMLLC owner's rights—both financial and management— and become the new owner/member of the SMLLC. Several other states, including Colorado, Arizona, and Maryland, have court cases that appear to give creditors more rights when dealing with owners of SMLLCs. This is an evolving area of law, and other states, too, may eventually have either court cases or statutes that would at least raise questions as to whether creditors have more rights when it comes to owners of SMLLCs.

At the same time, there are several states—such as Alaska, Delaware, Nevada, Oklahoma, South Dakota, and Wyoming—that have amended their LLC laws to make it clear that creditors do not have the right to anything more than a charging order for any LLC, including SMLLCs. Because these laws provide more protection from creditors, some people who are concerned about protecting their SMLLC assets from personal creditors may decide to form their SMLLC in one of these states if their home state has less favorable laws for SMLLC owners.

> **TIP**
>
> **The ULLCA addresses the issue of charging orders and asset protection in its explanatory comments.** One such comment states, "The charging order ... [as an exclusive remedy] was never intended to protect a ... debtor, but rather only to protect the interests of the ... debtor's co-owners." Another comment states "the charging order remedy was never intended as an 'asset protection' device for judgment debtors." The ULLCA comments, which seem to support a growing trend by some states to expand creditors' rights against SMLLC owners, include information about court cases involving owners of SMLLCs.

Foreclosure

Foreclosure gives a creditor more rights in a member's LLC interest than a charging order. Instead of just placing a lien on a member's LLC distributions, a foreclosure actually transfers the member's economic interest in the LLC to the creditor. A member's economic interest primarily includes the right to receive distributions from the LLC; it is specifically distinguished from a member's management interest, which gives a member the right to make decisions for the business.

Generally speaking, a creditor with the right to foreclose on an LLC membership interest does not have the right to make any management decisions for the business. However, in those states that allow foreclosure, the right to foreclose doesn't just give the creditor the right to receive all of a member's distributions (as with a charging order). Instead, at a minimum, a foreclosure order also gives the creditor the right to sell an LLC member's economic interest. In the case of SMLLCs, foreclosure occasionally may give a creditor even greater rights.

On its face, the right to foreclose might seem like a significant step up from a charging order. However, as a practical matter, it can be extremely difficult for a creditor to sell a member's economic interest.

For one thing, doing so usually requires the consent of all LLC members. Moreover, there may not be much value to an economic interest without a management interest—which often covers the right to make decisions about distributing LLC funds.

Roughly a third of the states explicitly allow personal creditors to foreclose on LLC interests. Many other states' laws are silent on the matter.

Currently, LLC laws in Florida and New Hampshire make the foreclosure option available in the case of SMLLCs but prohibit it for multi-member LLCs. Moreover, the rules in Florida and New Hampshire allow a personal creditor of an SMLLC member to obtain that member's entire interest in the SMLLC in a foreclosure, not just the member's economic interest. In addition, court cases involving an SMLLC member's bankruptcy, in states like Arizona, Colorado, and Maryland, have allowed bankruptcy trustees to obtain all of the single member's rights in the SMLLC, not just the member's economic rights. In these various states, the right to foreclose on an SMLLC membership interest can effectively be a right to dissolve the SMLLC.

Can I Add a Second Member to Avoid SMLLC Liability Issues?

Adding a second member to your LLC won't necessarily mean you will be treated as a multi-member LLC instead of an SMLLC by a court. You can't simply make a spouse, friend, or anyone else a member on paper to avoid the special liability risks associated with single-member LLCs. Instead, the second member must be a legitimate co-owner, which means the person must pay a fair price for membership and be given full financial and decision-making rights in the company. Otherwise, a court may well find that the second membership is a sham and treat the company as an SMLLC for liability purposes.

Dissolution

Here, dissolution means giving a personal creditor full control of an LLC, with the ability to sell off its assets and dissolve the company. Courts only very rarely give this kind of power to a personal creditor. However, as just mentioned, laws in Florida and New Hampshire allow creditors foreclosing on owners of SMLLCs to take all membership rights. In such cases, the creditor effectively could be placed in a position to dissolve the business. In addition, if an SMLLC owner declares bankruptcy, the SMLLC could be taken over by a bankruptcy trustee and dissolved as part of the bankruptcy process.

 CAUTION
Different rules apply if an SMLLC owner files for personal bankruptcy. A personal creditor usually goes after LLC assets when the member himself or herself doesn't have other personal assets to pay back what's due. Often, in such cases, the member ends up filing for personal bankruptcy. The rules for personal creditors in cases of bankruptcy are complex and go beyond the scope of this book. In general, however, bankruptcy usually involves the appointment of a third party—a bankruptcy trustee—who has broad powers over a debtor's assets, including LLC membership interests.

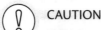 **CAUTION**
SMLLCs are sometimes promoted primarily as a method of asset protection. Some financial advisors may suggest that an SMLLC is a good place to park extra money. This book does not focus on SMLLCs as this sort of investment vehicle, but rather considers SMLLCs specifically as a way of forming and operating a small business. Looking at an SMLLC primarily as a place to stash personal assets rather than as a going concern can be a risky proposition and, in the event of a lawsuit by a personal creditor, may make it less likely that your assets really will be protected.

Running Your SMLLC: Additional Tasks

part from all the tasks related to forming your SMLLC, like filing articles of organization and preparing an operating agreement, there are various other matters you'll need to take care of when starting and running your new business. These include things like setting up a business bank account, filing annual reports, obtaining any necessary permits and licenses, and getting insurance. This chapter covers some of those additional tasks.

Establishing a Business Bank Account

The most important reason for opening a separate bank account for your business is to help ensure you have limited liability. As discussed earlier, your SMLLC by default is considered a legally separate entity from you, personally. That legal separation goes hand in hand with the protection from personal liability that the SMLLC provides. You could merely create an SMLLC on paper by filing articles of organization with the state and leave it at that. However, that likely won't be enough to definitively prove you and your SMLLC are separate and, by extension, ensure liability protection in the case of a lawsuit.

On the contrary, courts have consistently held that an LLC must take additional steps to demonstrate the distinction between the company and its owners. (This is covered more fully in Chapter 5.) One of the most important steps is separating an LLC's money from an owner's personal savings. As a rule, that means setting up a separate bank account for the business.

There are also other reasons why it makes sense to have at least one—and, for some businesses, more than one—business bank account. Briefly, a separate bank account:

- makes it easier to compute and pay taxes for your business
- makes you look more like a real, professional business as opposed to a small and potentially unreliable operation, and
- is useful, and may even be required, for accepting credit card payments.

You'll usually need just a few pieces of documentation to establish an SMLLC bank account. Namely:

- the company's EIN or other federal taxpayer ID number (TIN)
- a copy of the articles of organization (or, depending on the state where the SMLLC is organized, the equivalent document, such as a certificate of formation), and
- if the articles of organization do not provide sufficient information regarding who is authorized to sign on behalf of the SMLLC, an additional SMLLC document that does provide that information.

In short, you'll need basic documents that substantiate the name and general nature of your business. Regarding the last listed item, if the bank requires an additional document that shows you, specifically, are authorized to sign on behalf of your SMLLC, you can prepare a written resolution. (Written resolutions are covered in Chapter 7 and samples are included in the back of this book.)

CAUTION

Once you've set up your business bank account, use it only for business purposes. As covered in Chapter 5, you should use your business account only for business purposes and your personal bank account only for personal purposes. If you don't keep the uses separate, and instead commingle business and personal funds, you'll make it more likely you won't have limited liability in the event of a lawsuit.

Filing Annual Reports

Many states require that SMLLCs file annual reports. Annual reports generally are fairly simple documents that are used to reconfirm or, potentially, update basic information about your business. In most cases, this includes much of the same information that you must include in your original articles of organization. In other words, things like the name of your SMLLC, its principal office address, your name and address as the SMLLC's member, names and addresses of managers (if any), and the name and address of your registered agent. In many states, you also must pay an annual report filing fee. Depending on the state, the fee could range anywhere from under $20 to as high as $800 (California).

Due dates for annual reports can vary. In some states, the report is due during the anniversary month of your original filing of articles of organization. In other states, the report is due during the same period each year for all LLCs, regardless of when they originally filed articles of organization. In addition, many states have special rules about when the first annual report is due.

Some states will send out reminders to businesses before the annual report due date. If you fail to file your annual report when it's due, you usually are required to pay a penalty. Also, an increasing number of states now require that annual reports be filed online.

Copies of past annual reports usually are available online through your secretary of state's website. However, it can be helpful to have hard copies of these filings, including evidence of fee payments, at your place of business in the event there's a question regarding whether you have met your reporting obligations.

As a rule, if you stop filing annual reports for several years, the state will involuntarily dissolve your SMLLC. This is more technically known as administrative dissolution. If, for some reason, you find that your SMLLC has been administratively dissolved, there is usually a process to officially reinstate your company. However, reinstatement likely will be more costly than simply keeping up with annual report requirements. Also, after an administrative dissolution, you may lose the right to the name of your SMLLC.

> CAUTION
>
> **Administrative dissolution probably isn't the best way to close your SMLLC.** Technically you can close your business by simply stopping the filing of annual reports, and so eventually having your SMLLC administratively dissolved. However, this is not necessarily the recommended method. Instead, you should consider taking the formal, voluntary steps covered in Chapter 4. Among other concerns, an involuntary dissolution can leave you open to a variety of unexpected claims and a sudden loss of protection from personal liability.

Paying State LLC Taxes

Roughly a third of the states, including some of the most populous states, have tax rules that can or will require you to pay some amount of annual tax for your SMLLC. This is true in spite of the fact that, at least at the federal level, all SMLLCs by default are pass-through tax entities (see Chapter 2).

Among those states that directly tax LLCs, there is significant variation in how the tax is assessed. In some states, there is a flat annual tax on all LLCs. In recent years, the amount of different states' flat annual LLC taxes has ranged from $10 to $500. For example, in recent years a few New England states have imposed annual taxes ranging from $250 to $500.

Other states assess a tax based on a business's annual income or some aspect of a business's value. For example:

- New York and California both have a graduated tax that applies to all LLC income from in-state sources (including a minimum annual tax)
- Texas taxes LLCs with revenue exceeding roughly $1 million

- Ohio imposes a commercial activity tax (CAT) on gross receipts over $150,000
- Tennessee has both an excise tax on net earnings and a franchise tax on an LLC's net worth or tangible property, and
- Illinois has a tax related to an LLC's tangible personal property.

CAUTION
State LLC tax rules are subject to change. The rules for the example states mentioned in this section may change as time goes on. You should check the website for your state's tax agency (such as the Department of Revenue) for the most up-to-date information.

Business Permits and Licenses

Many businesses need permits or licenses in order to operate. Broadly speaking, these permits and licenses can be placed into one of two categories: regulatory or occupational.

Regulatory Permits and Licenses

Permits relating to things like health and safety, the environment, the sale or rental of certain products, and construction and zoning often are considered to be regulatory. Many regulatory permits and licenses are issued by state agencies, such as a department of environmental quality, department of agriculture, or department of revenue. State-issued regulatory permits and licenses may more specifically cover things like handling dangerous chemicals, collecting state sales tax, or operating a specific type of business (such as a child care facility).

Other regulatory permits are issued at the county or city level. Often, these locally issued permits relate to matters like zoning (allowing you to build or modify a certain kind of building in a certain location), maximum occupancy (for places like restaurants and bars), or public health (such as restaurant cleanliness). In addition, some cities, towns, and counties require businesses to obtain a general business license simply in order to operate in the locality. In some cases, these general licenses are related to paying local taxes. Those taxes may include local sales taxes.

It isn't always easy to figure out which regulatory permits your business needs. However, many state governments have websites covering many or all possible regulatory permits and licenses. In addition, a few states also have online questionnaires that allow you to provide basic information about your business and then receive a list of the particular permits or licenses you will need. At the local level, many cities, towns, and counties also have websites with sections devoted to local regulatory permits. Checking these state and local websites usually is the quickest way to discover any local permits required for your business.

Many business permits and licenses must be kept at your place of business. In addition, some permits and licenses must be posted in a certain location.

> **EXAMPLE:** Daryl has organized his small food truck business as a New York SMLLC. He will operate in Brooklyn and sell food that he and his assistant prepare. He will also sell beverages including beer. He uses a website maintained by the State of New York that deals specifically with state-issued regulatory permits and licenses. The website allows him to complete a basic questionnaire about his business. The website then provides him with a list of state-issued permits and licenses he'll need for his business. The list includes links to the forms he'll need to complete in order to obtain those licenses and permits. Daryl also uses a website maintained by New York City's Department of Health to get information about additional local licenses and certificates he will need. From these two websites, he learns that, among other things, he'll have to file registrations related to mobile food vending, the sale of alcohol, collection of sales tax, and employer obligations.

Occupational Licenses and Certifications

Occupational licenses and certifications (which include professional licenses) are issued by state agencies and regulatory boards. You'll need one of these licenses or certificates in order to engage in any of an array of different occupations or professions. The exact occupations and professions requiring licensing or certification are defined by each individual state's laws.

In some cases, a required license or certificate will be issued by a centralized office of the state government. In other cases, the license will be issued by a separate regulatory board or agency. The latter situation most often applies to those occupations that are considered professions (like physicians, surgeons, attorneys, accountants, dentists, and architects).

Apart from individual regulatory boards and agencies for particular occupations and professions, most states also have a central state office that supervises all of these various boards and agencies. The office may be a division within the secretary of state, department of labor, or another major state agency. By going to the website for the supervisory office, you should be able to find a list of most or all licensed occupations and professions in your state. These online lists usually contain links that take you directly to the website for the specific regulatory board or agency that actually handles the licensing for a particular occupation or profession. In turn, the board and agency websites usually provide a detailed explanation of how to apply for the relevant license or certificate, including copies of forms and information about fees.

EXAMPLE: Jeff recently started thinking about creating an SMLLC to provide licensed real estate appraisal services. However, he wants to find out whether there are any occupational licensing requirements, and, if so, what those requirements are. His state government has an Office of Occupational Regulation. By going to the office's website, he finds a list of several dozen state-regulated occupations and professions—including real estate appraisers. By clicking on the real estate appraisers link, he is taken to the website for the state's Real Estate Appraiser Board. (He also could have done an Internet search for real estate appraiser licensing that might have taken him directly to the board's website.) The board website gives him all the details about how to apply for a real estate appraiser's license.

Fictitious or Assumed Name (DBA) Certificates

You can operate your business under a different name than what's registered in your articles of organization. Depending on where you're doing business, this alternative business name technically may be known as an assumed name, a fictitious name, a DBA (for "doing business as"), or a trade name. Often an assumed or fictitious name will omit the suffix "LLC" or "Limited Liability Company" that is required for the official name you originally register for your SMLLC.

As with the official name you registered in your articles of organization, assumed or fictitious names are subject to trademark laws. As discussed more fully in Chapter 3, that means you must avoid using assumed or fictitious names that are the same as or similar to names already being used by other businesses.

In most states, you must register an SMLLC's assumed or fictitious name with the secretary of state. In a few states, you must register with the county clerk in each county where your SMLLC will do business.

You generally are required to pay a fee when you first register an assumed or fictitious business name. In addition, assumed and fictitious names generally expire after a number of years, at which point you must renew the name, including paying a renewal fee.

You should keep a copy of any assumed or fictitious name certificate in a safe place. In case of a dispute, you might need the certificate to clarify the naming situation for your business.

EXAMPLE: The articles of organization for Mandy's SMLLC show her true business name is "Other Side of the Fence Lawn Care, L.L.C." However, she wants her website, business cards, and trucks to display the name "Greener Grass Landscaping." After checking to make sure no one else is using a similar name, she goes to the website for the secretary of state and downloads an application for an assumed business name. She completes the form and submits it to the secretary of state along with a check for the application fee. After she receives confirmation that her application is accepted, she can start operating as Greener Grass Landscaping. She keeps a copy of the assumed name confirmation in a safe place with her other important business documents.

Trademarks and Service Marks

There are separate legal definitions for trademarks and service marks. However, speaking very generally, trademarks and service marks are used to uniquely identify, respectively, goods (products) and services. This particularly includes distinguishing a product or service from competitors. (Trade names, which have some legal similarities to trademarks and in certain circumstances can become trademarks, often are considered to be the same as or similar to assumed or fictitious business names; the latter types of names are discussed in the preceding section.)

You can register trademarks and service marks both with the United States Patent and Trademark Office (USPTO) and with individual states. Registering a trademark or service mark may put you in a better position to defend your product or service from unfair competition. For example, you might manufacture and sell a popular and unique toy. The toy might have a particular design and be sold under a distinctive name. If someone else starts producing and selling cheap copies of the toy with essentially the same design and using a similar name, that might constitute trademark infringement. You might have a stronger case for blocking the infringing competitor if you previously had registered your toy's design and name with the USPTO.

EXAMPLE: Carlotta formed her SMLLC to make and sell candy. She wants to sell a new coffee-cocoa candy bar under the name "Carl's Koko Moka Bzzz Bar," which is printed in a unique typeface and includes a unique logo showing stylized chocolate and coffee beans. So—after checking to make sure the name, typeface, and logo aren't already in use—she goes to the USPTO website. On the website, she can complete and file an online trademark application including paying the filing fee. The USPTO will review her application and, hopefully, within about three months, Carlotta will receive confirmation that her trademark (the product name, typeface, and logo) have been accepted and registered. At that point, she can feel more confident about stopping other people from trying to sell knockoffs of her candy bar.

The example is very simple and intended only to give you a general idea of how a trademark registration might work. Also, this section does not touch on patents, which, along with copyright, is another major area of intellectual property (or IP) protection. You can find much more information about trademarks, service marks, trade names, and patents from other Nolo books. Start by looking at *Trademark: Legal Care for Your Business & Product Name* and *Patent, Copyright & Trademark: An Intellectual Property Desk Reference*, both by Richard Stim.

Liability Insurance

Forming your business as an SMLLC will protect you personally from many kinds of liability. However, the company itself remains vulnerable in the event of business-related accidents. Therefore, most SMLLCs should have at least some liability insurance. Without it, a single unfortunate accident could lead to damages that would bankrupt your business.

General Liability Policies

If your business has even minimal direct contact with customers or clients, you should have a general liability policy. Imagine that a customer or client suffers bodily injury while on your business premises, such as in your office or store, or because of the negligence of one of your employees while the employee is working outside of your principal place of business. In such cases, the injured person may be able to collect for medical bills, lost wages, pain and suffering, and other items. Moreover, apart from physical injuries, your business also may be liable for damages for such things as libel, slander, false arrest, and false imprisonment.

General liability policies provide coverage for judgments relating to these types of injury lawsuits up to the limits of the policy, as well as covering the cost of defending the lawsuits. The policies cover a range of possible injuries to your clients or customers; for example, slipping and falling at your place of business, or otherwise being harmed by a physical object located on your business premises. (Note, however, that some amounts awarded in lawsuits usually won't be covered by a general liability policy—such as if your business is required to pay punitive damages for willful or malicious actions.)

General liability policies typically have dollar limits for each incident, as well as an overall limit for the policy year. For example, a policy may pay up to $1,000,000 per claim and up to a total of $3,000,000 for the policy year.

If your SMLLC leases its space from someone else, the building owner likely will have liability insurance. However, you can and should still have your own general liability policy.

Product Liability Insurance

If your SMLLC designs, manufactures, or sells products, you should seriously consider getting product liability insurance. This is insurance that covers your business in the event a person is injured by a product that is defective or lacks adequate safety warnings or instructions.

While product liability insurance is expensive, you need to consider the potential cost of going without. More particularly, if you manufacture items that clearly may injure people, such as chemicals or construction equipment, product liability insurance is worth the cost. However, if you're a retailer selling products packaged by the manufacturer, and you do not service, assemble, or provide advice regarding the products, your potential liability is far more limited, with the manufacturer generally bearing most of the legal responsibility. Consequently, you may well have adequate coverage under your general liability policy.

Determining the appropriate amount of product liability insurance will depend largely on what kind of product you're dealing with. A company that manufactures spiral-bound notebooks and has five million dollars in annual sales should not need as much coverage as a company that manufactures artificial knees and also has five million dollars in annual sales.

Vehicle Insurance

Your business's vehicle insurance should cover not only cars and trucks owned by the business, but also those belonging to your employees, to the extent the employees' vehicles are being used for business purposes. This type of employee-vehicle insurance, technically known as "employer's non-owned automobile liability insurance," is generally not very expensive, and usually is worth the cost. The coverage it provides is not included under a general liability policy.

While you may want to investigate employees' driving records before sending them out in company vehicles or on company business in their own vehicles, a failure to check should not be a problem under most policies. One exception would be where the insurer has specifically excluded an employee from coverage. This may result from your providing the names of employees you want covered to the insurance company, and the insurance company checking the employees' driving records and finding a bad driving record for a particular employee.

Also, if your company leases vehicles, you should be able to add coverage for injury or property damage under either your vehicle insurance policy or your general liability policy. (This is referred to as "hired vehicle" coverage.)

Workers' Compensation Insurance

Workers' compensation insurance covers injuries to employees, and all businesses with employees are required by law to have this type of insurance. Workers' compensation insurance protects your business from being sued for negligence with regard to its employees. Instead of a lawsuit, employees injured on the job receive compensation for costs associated with their injuries through your business's workers' compensation insurance.

In order to make a workers' comp claim, the basic rule is that an employee has to have been injured in the course of employment. This rule can be interpreted quite broadly; for example, it may include employees injured at social functions associated with your business.

The specific requirements for obtaining workers' compensation insurance vary on a state-by-state basis. Most small businesses pay money into a state-run fund or get a policy through a private insurance company. "Self-insuring" requires you to keep large amounts of cash in reserve and, at least for small businesses, generally isn't a realistic option.

Your rates for worker's compensation insurance will vary depending on what kind of business you're in. More dangerous businesses, such as working with hazardous chemicals, will have higher rates than lower-risk businesses, such as offices that provide business services. Your business's safety record may also be taken into account when computing rates.

Be aware that standard workers' compensation insurance might not cover every type of harm an employee may experience while on the job. More specifically, an employee may be able to sue in court for injuries resulting from gross negligence or intentional conduct. You should obtain separate workers' compensation insurance to cover these types of claims.

Finally, be aware that workers' compensation insurance is not required for independent contractors. However, you should make sure that you accurately distinguish between independent contractors and employees. If you do not provide workers' comp coverage to a person doing work for you because you wrongly think he or she is an independent contractor rather than an employee, and then that person is injured on the job, you may be on the hook for a large settlement.

Professional Liability Insurance

If you're a licensed professional, then you probably are already familiar with professional liability insurance, also commonly known as malpractice insurance. It covers you in the event you make a serious mistake in the practice of your profession and are sued by a patient or client. As with general liability policies, professional liability policies generally have dollar limits for each incident and an overall limit for the policy year. Both when you originally apply for professional liability insurance, and each subsequent year when you renew your policy, you usually will have to answer questions about the specific nature of your professional practice—such as what specific areas you practice in.

CAUTION

You should keep copies of all your business insurance documents in a safe location. In case of an incident that might be covered by a policy—a fire, an on-site injury to a customer, an unforeseen event that results in a broken contract, a client's lawsuit—you'll want quick access to the details of your coverage.

Doing Business in Other States

There are various situations in which you may find yourself doing business in other states. Common examples include:

- organizing your SMLLC in one state but having your principal location in another state
- selling products over state lines via the Internet, phone, or regular mail, or
- organizing your SMLLC in one state but later expanding into other states.

In order to do business in states other than the one in which you organized your SMLLC, you may have to go through a registration process in those other states. This process is referred to as qualifying or registering to do business in another state.

In general, whether you'll be required to register with another state depends on whether you are engaged in so-called intrastate business within that state. (This is sometimes more simply and ambiguously referred to as "doing business in" the state.) That generally means you have some kind of physical presence in the state. Physical presence might take the form of a building, such as an office or a warehouse, or possibly an employee who works in that state. As a rule, if you are engaged in intrastate business in a state, you must register with that state. Unfortunately, states often don't provide detailed definitions of what does and does not constitute doing business in the state for registration purposes, and sometimes it can be difficult to know whether a given situation requires registration. If you are doing more than just shipping products through third-party carriers to customers in another state, you may want to consult with a lawyer in that state for an opinion on whether registration is necessary.

> CAUTION
>
> **Some business-related activities in another state don't constitute intrastate business.** Examples of activities that typically are considered exempt include: maintaining a bank account in the state; making sales or taking orders by phone or mail; including the state in a national ad campaign; using independent contractors to make sales in the state; or having a website that's accessible in the state. If your SMLLC's connection to another state is limited to these kinds of activities, you generally are not required to register with that state.

> CAUTION
>
> **The law has changed regarding sales tax on Internet sales to other states.** In 2018, the United States Supreme Court fundamentally changed the rules for collection of sales tax by Internet-based sellers. In its decision in *South Dakota v. Wayfair Inc.*, the Court effectively stated that individual states can require online sellers to collect state sales tax on their sales. This ruling overturns the old rule established in 1992. The old rule prohibited states from requiring a business to collect sales tax unless the business had a physical presence in the state. After *Wayfair*, sales tax rules are in flux. If your SMLLC sells products to other states, you should keep an eye on sales tax laws for the states where your customers are located—and on any new federal laws regarding sales tax.

To qualify to do business in another state, you must complete and file a form similar to the articles of organization you filed when you first created your SMLLC. Depending on the state, the form might be called something like "Application for Registration of Foreign Limited Liability Company" or "Application for Authority to Transact Business of Foreign Limited Liability Company." One distinct item on these applications is the name and street address of a registered agent in the state you're applying to. This will be different from the information for the registered agent in the state where you originally organized your SMLLC. More specifically, you must have a separate registered agent for the state you're applying to and that agent must be located in that other state.

TIP

When completing an application to do business in another state, the term "foreign" doesn't mean a non-American company. Rather, in this case "foreign" means an LLC or other form of business that was organized in a state other than the one you're now applying to. For example, an LLC organized in Iowa is a foreign LLC in Indiana.

You must pay a fee to file an application to do business in another state. The fee will vary from one state to the next, but generally will be between $100 and $500.

Part of being registered to do business in another state means that you must properly report and pay all of the relevant taxes required by that state. Depending on what you're doing in the state, that might include paying sales taxes, income taxes, property taxes, and payroll taxes.

Failure to register your SMLLC with another state when you're legally required to do so can have various unpleasant consequences. At a minimum, you may be subject to late filing penalties. Depending on the state, those penalties can be pricey. In addition, you likely will be prohibited from bringing a lawsuit in the state's courts. A defendant in the state usually can ask a court to dismiss such a lawsuit on the basis that your business was not properly registered (qualified) with the state.

You can get more detailed information on this topic from the Nolo book *How to Do Business Outside Your State*, by Anthony Mancuso and Rich Stim.

Employees

There are a large number of potential issues related to hiring employees for your SMLLC. Among the most important general issues are:

- hiring, including advertising and describing jobs, holding interviews, and making job offers, complying with immigration law requirements, and reporting hires to the state
- personnel practices, including employee files, employee handbooks, and disciplining employees

- dealing with employee benefits, including things like health care coverage and retirement plans
- providing family and medical leave
- managing employee health and safety, including complying with federal and state OSHA laws, and dealing with things like workers' compensation and hazardous chemicals
- avoiding illegal discrimination
- terminating employees, including avoidance of wrongful terminations
- employee privacy, and
- using independent contractors, including avoiding improper classification of employees as independent contractors and vice versa.

Apart from certain employee taxation issues, which are covered in Chapter 2, employee issues are beyond the scope of this book. For complete coverage of all important employee issues, get *The Employer's Legal Handbook: Manage Your Employees & Workplace Effectively* (Nolo), by Fred S. Steingold. ●

Financial Record Keeping and Written Resolutions

Ｔhe day-to-day running of any SMLLC includes keeping records. Many of these records relate to finances (including taxes). However, you'll want to make sure you keep good records of other types of documents, as well, such as organizational and management documents, government-issued certificates and licenses, statements of formal business decisions, contracts, and copies of administrative filings. This chapter covers the most common ongoing record-keeping requirements for an SMLLC.

Financial Record Keeping

The financial records you'll need to have will include the payments your business receives from customers or clients, and the payments your business makes to pay its bills. In other words, at a minimum you'll need to keep records of income and expenses. Depending on what kind of business you have, expenses could include a wide range of things, from supplies, equipment, and inventory to rent, utility bills, and employee salaries. In addition, you also may need to keep records of loan payments, insurance payments, and other important transactions with financial institutions, insurance companies, or other entities. Your income records, too, might be somewhat complicated, particularly if you receive payments subject to sales or excise taxes, or if you receive interim payments under contracts. And speaking of taxes, apart from income and expense records, you'll also need to keep copies of federal and state tax returns, and possibly estimated tax payments, employer tax payments, and other tax filings.

In spite of the potentially complicated nature of some businesses' finances, you're usually not legally required to keep your records, financial or otherwise, in any specific form. For example, if you wanted, you could throw copies of all your bills and receipts into a shoebox. However, even for the smallest SMLLCs, at least a slightly more organized approach is advisable. One of the simplest ways to keep at least some financial records is to use the register of your business checkbook. Just as when you write checks and make deposits in your personal checking account, and then record each of those transactions in your checkbook register, you can also record that same basic information for your SMLLC in the business checkbook's register.

However, while using a business checkbook register is simple, by itself it often isn't sufficient for handling many basic but important details of business finances. There are often documents you will want to retain which show specific information about individual transactions. For many businesses, two obvious examples are copies of bills your business sends out to customers or clients, and copies of bills your business receives from creditors. In many cases, you'll want to refer back to these various bills for additional information; just knowing the amounts you received or paid won't be enough.

With this in mind, a further simple idea for financial record keeping is to use two sets of file folders: one set for income you receive and one set for expenses you pay. You can write the name of a single client or creditor on each individual folder, put bills for each client or creditor in the proper folder, and then put each set of folders in its own file drawer or banker's box. Alternatively, if your business is small enough, or has few enough transactions, you might be able to forgo file folders, and instead use one or two three-ring binders, or even a few large envelopes, to store copies of bills and similar documents.

If your business deals with multiple customers on a daily basis—such as a retail store or a restaurant—you'll need a system to handle daily receipts. Once again, a checkbook register alone likely won't be enough to cover even basic record keeping for these types of businesses. Instead, you may need other documentation—even something as simple as information written on deposit receipts issued by your bank—where you break down the various items involved in each deposit. In addition, it is often worthwhile to maintain monthly and annual summaries of cash receipts, which can be helpful for financial analysis and planning.

Sample Daily Sales Summary

Retail Store						
Item Name	Item No.	Unit Price	Quantity	Sales	Sales Tax	Total
Teacups	11111	$5.00	25	$125.00	$6.25	$131.25
Candles	22222	$2.50	48	$120.00	$6.00	$126.00
Candy Bars	33333	$4.00	50	$200.00	$10.00	$210.00
Mugs	44444	$6.00	32	$192.00	$9.60	$201.60
Soaps	55555	$3.00	45	$135.00	$6.75	$141.75
Sweaters	66666	$30.00	10	$300.00	$15.00	$315.00
Teapots	77777	$12.00	7	$84.00	$4.20	$88.20
					Total	$1,213.80
Form of Payment						
					Cash	$501.30
					Credit Card	$602.50
					ApplePay	$110.00
					Total	$1,213.80
					Over/Short	$0.00

If your business has employees, you'll also need to deal with an additional level of record keeping. Paying employees isn't simply one more business expense. On the contrary, there are special tax issues, including withholding and deductions that apply only to salaries and not other types of expenses. Tracking employee compensation often includes recording each employee's hours worked, total pay, deductions, and then monthly gross payroll. In short, you may find you'll want a third set of file folders, or a third binder or envelope, specifically to track employee pay and related employment matters.

TIP

Employee taxation issues are covered in more detail in Chapter 2.
There you'll find information about withholding taxes and unemployment
insurance taxes.

Good financial record keeping also extends to your business's
property. Ideally, your records regarding property will include:

- when and how you acquired an item, including the price paid
  (often available from a sales receipt)
- for things like office space or real estate, the cost of any
  improvements (again, often available from a receipt from, for
  example, a contractor), and
- any deductions related to depreciation (which is a method for
  paying taxes on durable property).

The last issue, depreciation, which commonly involves spreading
out taxes on durable property over a period of years, is a tax topic unto
itself that in some cases can be complicated. Additional information
is available in Nolo books (such as *Tax Savvy for Small Business,* by
Frederick Daily and Jeffrey Quinn) and in articles in the Taxes and
Small Business sections of Nolo's website.

TIP

Consider storing additional document copies electronically.
Having hard copies of important documents, particularly those with original
signatures, can be crucial. However, it's often a good idea to also store additional
copies in electronic format. Two common options are an external hard drive or
an Internet cloud service. Electronic storage generally is both cheap and easy.
Just be very careful that any electronic storage method you use is password-
protected and otherwise reasonably secure.

Sample Monthly Profit and Loss Report

Income	
Sales	$10,000.00
Services	$15,000.00
Other Income	$1,000.00
Total Income	**$26,000.00**
Expenses	
Advertising	$2,000.00
Bank charges	$100.00
Car and truck expenses	$500.00
Commissions and fees	$300.00
Contract labor	$500.00
Cost of goods sold	$1,000.00
Insurance	$200.00
Interest: Mortgage (paid to banks, etc.)	$1,000.00
Legal and professional services	$1,200.00
Office expense	$2,000.00
Professional training	$1,000.00
Rent and leases: Vehicles, machinery, and equipment	$2,500.00
Repairs and maintenance	$600.00
Supplies	$400.00
Taxes and licenses	$50.00
Travel, meals, and entertainment	$200.00
Utilities	$650.00
Wages	$3,000.00
Other expenses	$1,000.00
Total Expenses	**$18,200.00**
Net Income (Loss)	**$6,800.00**

> **TIP**
>
> **Home office expenses include bills that are not explicitly business-related.** Many SMLLCs are run out of home offices—a spare bedroom, space in a basement or a garage, even a walk-in closet. If you have a home office, you can deduct a portion of some of your household expenses—such as home utility bills—from your SMLLC taxes as a business expense. Therefore, it's important to keep records of household expenses that apply to your home office. Consider making copies of those bills and putting them in the files containing the rest of your business expenses.

With all the latter points in mind, here's a brief word about book-keeping software. While certainly not required, these programs often can make record keeping much easier. They can, of course, help with keeping accurate records and reconciling your checkbook. They also can help you create financial reports that run the gamut from simple (a list of bank transactions for the last 30 days) to sophisticated (profit and loss statements, balance sheets, expense category charts, and so on). These reports can be extremely useful for analyzing your business (where's money coming from, where's it going, and how you might be able to spend less or earn more). They can also make filing your taxes a much faster process.

> **CAUTION**
>
> **You are required to keep copies of your SMLLC's tax records.** Under IRS rules, you must retain different tax records for different periods of time. In many cases, the period is three years. However, if you have employees, you must keep all employment tax records for at least four years after the date the relevant employment taxes were paid. Furthermore, in certain situations, if you previously have failed to properly report income on a tax return, you may be required to maintain records going back six years. And for business property, including depreciable items, you generally must keep property records until you dispose of the property. Also, bear in mind that you may need to keep certain records longer than required by the IRS; for example, an insurance company or a creditor may need you to hold certain documents longer than is needed for tax purposes.

TIP

Securities laws and filings probably won't come into play. Membership interests in a multi-member LLC sometimes are considered securities, similar to more familiar investment vehicles like stocks and bonds, and are subject to securities laws. However, for an SMLLC, which by definition has only one member, securities laws generally do not apply and you won't have to deal with the related securities record keeping.

What If I'm Operating at a Loss?

There's no inherent shame—and there shouldn't be any legal problems—if your SMLLC is temporarily operating at a loss. In general, operating at a loss means your business pays out more in expenses than it takes in as income. That can happen for a number of legitimate reasons. You might just have a bad year with relatively low sales or few clients. Another possibility is that you pay a lot for new equipment this year because your business is rapidly expanding, but you fully expect to return to profitability next year.

Whatever the reason, when operating at a loss there are two important points to keep in mind. First, federal and state tax systems are fully able to accommodate businesses that operate at a loss. For a typical SMLLC, a loss will show up on federal Schedule C after subtracting all expenses from all sources of income. That loss then gets carried over to your personal Form 1040. You can find more details in Chapter 2.

The second important point is that operating at a loss does not relieve you of the obligation to ensure your SMLLC is adequately capitalized. As discussed elsewhere in this book, state LLC laws typically require that you have adequate capitalization—that is, have enough money available to cover reasonable near-term expenses. You may not make a profit during the year, but you still should keep at least some cash on hand. An SMLLC with no money in the bank and no real assets is at risk for being considered a sham entity. In such cases, a court might decide that you, as the sole owner, are personally liable for the SMLLC's debts and other liabilities.

Other Records

Records of income and expenses, and other financial and tax documents, are not the only papers you need to keep for your SMLLC. There are a variety of other documents, including some relating to state and local government agencies, that you should maintain in your business records. Here's a quick look at some of the most important ones.

Operating agreement. Most states' LLC laws require that you keep a copy of your operating agreement at your primary place of business. Beyond the legal requirement, it's simply a good idea to have this document readily available in case any questions ever arise about the official rules for running your company. In addition, some banks and businesses will require a copy of the operating agreement in order to do business with you.

Articles of organization. The original copy of your articles of organization (or equivalent document) is kept on file by the secretary of state (or equivalent state office). Moreover, you can often view a copy of the document by going online to your secretary of state's website. However, it's a good idea to have a physical copy in your records that you can quickly access and review.

Certificate of good standing. Most states will issue a certificate of good standing to a business upon request. The certificate essentially indicates that you've been filing any required annual reports and paying all required state taxes. Before doing business with your SMLLC, some banks and businesses will require a current certificate of good standing in addition to a copy of your operating agreement.

Annual reports. It can be helpful to have hard copies of your annual report filings, including evidence of fee payments, at your place of business in the event there's a question regarding whether you have met your reporting obligations.

Fictitious or assumed name (DBA) certificates. If you've filed with a state or local government office to operate your business under an assumed name, you should keep a copy of the DBA certificate. In case of a dispute, you might need the certificate to clarify the naming situation for your business.

Business licenses and permits. State and federal laws often require that government-issued licenses, permits, and certificates be kept at your place of business. You may even be required to display certain government notices in a conspicuous location.

Insurance documents. You should keep copies of all your business insurance documents in a safe location. In case of an incident that might be covered by your policy—a fire, an on-site injury to a customer, an unforeseen event that results in a broken contract—you'll want quick access to the details of your coverage.

Contracts. If your business does its work through contracts, you'll certainly want to maintain a safe file where those contracts are kept. As with certain other records, they can become very important in the event of a dispute.

Promissory notes. If your SMLLC has lent money under a promissory note, make sure the note is stored in a safe but readily accessible location. The note is your primary evidence that the borrower owes your company money. It's also a negotiable instrument, meaning it is similar to a check or cash, so you should treat it with care similar to that used with other money.

Capital contributions and withdrawals. In many cases, your operating agreement will include a statement of the initial capital contribution (investment of money, property, or services) into your SMLLC. However, if you do not have an operating agreement, or if you make additional investments into the company or take out some portion of capital, you should keep records of those transactions.

Employer identification number (EIN). As discussed in the chapter on SMLLC formation, many SMLLCs, including those with employees and those choosing to be taxed as corporations, will have EINs. You should keep a copy of the IRS form issuing your EIN in a handy location.

 CAUTION

Be careful when you sign documents on behalf of your SMLLC. Whenever you sign contracts, forms, applications, or other documents for your business, you should make clear you're doing so only as a representative of your company. Typically, this means printing the name of your SMLLC above your signature, and then, below your signature, printing your name, a comma, and a term or phrase such as "Member." Signing this way will help you maintain limited liability protection by making it clear that your SMLLC is separate from you, personally, and that only the company, and not you, is being committed by your signature.

SMLLC Meetings and Resolutions

Part of the attraction of an LLC, as opposed to a corporation, is the relative informality of management. In most states, formal member meetings aren't legally required for LLCs. However, it is not uncommon for a multi-member LLC to provide for member meetings in its operating agreement. Often, two types of meetings are mentioned: annual (or otherwise regularly scheduled) meetings and special meetings. Special meetings are usually called when the company must take urgent action. Member meetings typically are used to make major decisions for a company. Someone at the meeting records minutes (a summary) of what happened, including the date, starting and ending times, who was in attendance, and what was discussed. When decisions are made (typically through a member or manager vote), they are noted in the minutes, and also are sometimes documented in the form of written consent actions or resolutions which are attached to the meeting minutes. The meeting minutes, including any attached resolutions, are filed in a meeting minutes binder.

In the world of multi-member LLCs, member meetings give all members, including those who may not be routinely involved in the running of the company, an opportunity to participate in major decision making. In the world of SMLLCs, however, this reason for holding a member meeting loses much of its relevance. Because an SMLLC has just a single member, who in turn usually is running the company, there often is no issue of notifying other people about big decisions. (If there's any question about this, you usually can help ensure that formalities regarding notice are not legally necessary by including relevant language in your SMLLC's operating agreement; that language will supersede default provisions in your state's LLC laws.) For the same reason, no general agreement or majority vote is necessary for a decision to be made. On the contrary, in many cases, single members will simply decide by themselves what they want to do and then do it.

Similarly, consent actions and resolutions can seem to make more sense for multi-member LLCs than for SMLLCs. For multi-member LLCs, a primary purpose of resolutions is to give all members a document to refer to in case they later find themselves in disagreement. For an SMLLC, however, there is just one member, and so a disagreement, at least among members, is not possible.

There are, however, other reasons why it might be useful for your SMLLC to hold meetings or at least use written resolutions. First, by observing these kinds of formalities, you might help protect the limited liability status of your company if it comes under scrutiny in court. Strictly speaking, courts generally are more concerned about "economic separation" of an SMLLC from its owner, and not about whether the company closely observes "corporate formalities" (tasks legally required of corporations, but not LLCs, like holding annual shareholder meetings and keeping meeting minutes). In other words, courts would look at whether you are using your SMLLC's checking account to pay personal expenses, or using a truck registered to your SMLLC mainly for personal road trips, but would not be particularly concerned that meetings aren't being held and major decisions aren't being documented. Nevertheless, even for an SMLLC, a court might take into account formalities such as meetings and resolutions in deciding whether the company was truly separate from its single owner, and whether the owner is entitled to limited liability protection.

Second, there may be cases where an outside party, such as a lender, an insurance company, a real estate management company, or government agency, would ask that you produce a written resolution as proof that you have authority to take certain significant action for your company. While a copy of an operating agreement often will suffice, in cases where there is no operating agreement, or for certain types of transactions (for example, a sale or purchase of real estate), a specific, written resolution may be required.

Third, your SMLLC may rely on the help of outside advisers, such as attorneys, accountants, financial consultants, or other experts, when making business decisions. On some occasions, you may want to hold a formal meeting that includes one or more of these other people. In those instances, even though the other people won't have the authority of a company member, it nonetheless can be useful to keep meeting minutes so everyone has a record of what was discussed.

As a final reason, if you hope to attract outside investment in your business, keeping written records of major decisions may help show potential investors that you're taking your business seriously.

To be clear, most business decisions, including day-to-day decisions, are made without resolutions or other documentation. With an SMLLC, you'd only use a resolution to document the most important business matters or actions such as:

- buying or selling real estate
- getting a loan, establishing a bank account, or otherwise working with a financial institution
- amending the articles of organization or operating agreement
- approving a major contract with a client or supplier
- delegating specific authority to another person or authorizing a person to take a specific action, and
- adding one or more members to the company.

The content of a resolution is flexible and, of course, will vary depending on what action is being taken. For example, a resolution to sell real estate typically would include the property address, the price and other terms of the sale, and a statement that someone (such as the single member of the SMLLC) is authorized to execute all documents necessary to complete the transaction under the stated terms.

 TIP
You can find sample written resolutions at the back of this book. The sample resolutions include sample written consents by a sole member granting or rescinding authority to take certain actions on behalf of an SMLLC, like opening a bank account or purchasing property. Use them to help guide you when you need to prepare your own resolutions.

Why Keep Good Records?

The preceding sections show that keeping clear, organized records for your SMLLC can be useful for at least three reasons:
- it helps with filing your taxes
- it can help in dealing with lenders and other businesses, and
- it might help establish that your business is separate from you personally.

Here's a brief review each of these points.

Preparing Your Taxes

One of the most important reasons to keep clear financial records is to make it easier for you to compute and pay your business's taxes. The typical SMLLC is taxed as a sole proprietorship, which means you'll pay taxes on your business income as part of your personal income tax return. This involves completing a Schedule C that breaks down your SMLLC's income and, especially, expenses into various categories. These categories include things like equipment, supplies, advertising, and rent.

If you've kept clear, organized financial records during the year, it should be relatively easy to plug in the right numbers for each category.

Some businesses use items, most often equipment or machinery, that are subject to depreciation. Part of good record keeping as it relates to taxes means keeping up to date with how much a given piece of business property has depreciated. Again, when tax time rolls around, you'll save yourself a lot of aggravation if you have a file folder or binder section where you have documents tracking equipment depreciation.

Clear, well-organized records also can be one of your best defenses in the event the IRS audits your business. If, for example, the IRS questions a particular business expense—say, the purchase of a delivery vehicle—you'll be in a much better position if you can show things like a purchase receipt, insurance documents including payment records, the vehicle title and registration in the name of your SMLLC, and a document showing the sales tax paid on the purchase. All of this could be kept in a single folder among your business records. (Of course, as mentioned earlier, under IRS rules you also should have copies of tax returns going back a minimum of three years that you could produce upon request.)

Working With Lenders

Let's say that your SMLLC has been humming along successfully for a few years and now you want to expand the business. Maybe you need some new equipment; maybe you want to buy some real estate for a store or office. If your business itself doesn't have the money for these types of purchases, you'll probably need to get a loan. Banks, as well as many other lenders, won't make loans without security. In other words, a bank will want your business to put up some kind of collateral that the bank can take possession of if you're unable to keep up with your loan payments. A bank will want to see clear and detailed records regarding not only your business's income and expenses (a profit and loss statement, a balance sheet), but also records showing the SMLLC's ownership of property or other items that may be used as collateral.

In addition, even before applying for a loan, good financial records will allow you, possibly with the help of a financial expert, to analyze whether getting a loan is a good move at a particular point in time. The same records also can help you to analyze what size loan might make sense. And, finally, they can also be useful for helping you determine the tax implications of a loan.

Helping Prove Your SMLLC Is Separate From Yourself

As mentioned throughout this book, one of the main benefits of organizing your small business as an SMLLC is to gain the protection of limited liability. If your business has debts it can't pay, or is responsible for a serious injury to a customer or client, limited liability means that no one can come after you, personally, for compensation. However, if it is not clear that your SMLLC is truly a separate entity from you, a court might allow someone to pierce your business's limited liability shield. While courts are mainly concerned that you keep your company's money and property separate from your personal assets, keeping separate records may also help. More specifically, as long as your SMLLC is adequately capitalized—that is, has enough money or other assets to continue paying its ongoing financial obligations—then clear business records might help defeat a legal challenge to the idea that your business is separate from you. ●

Sample Operating Agreement
for a California Single-Member Limited
Liability Company (Manager-Managed)

Operating Agreement of Fit, LLC, a California Single-Member Limited Liability Company (Manager-Managed)

1. Preliminary Provisions

a. Effective Date

This operating agreement of Fit, LLC, effective as of the date signed below, is adopted by the member whose signature appears at the end of this agreement.

b. Formation

This limited liability company (LLC) was formed by filing its articles of organization, certificate of organization, or certificate of formation with the California Secretary of State or other LLC filings office.

The legal existence of this LLC commenced on the date of such filing. A copy of this organizational document will be placed in the LLC's records book.

c. Name

The formal name of this LLC is as stated above. However, this LLC may do business under a different name by complying with California's fictitious or assumed business name statutes and procedures.

d. Registered Office and Registered Agent

The LLC may change its registered office and/or agent from time to time by filing a change of registered agent or office statement with the California Secretary of State or other LLC filings office.

e. Business Purpose

The specific business purposes and activities of this LLC at the time of initial signing of this agreement consist of the following:

To operate a group fitness membership-based gym.

It is understood that the foregoing statement of powers shall not serve as a limitation on the powers or abilities of this LLC, which shall be permitted to engage in any and all lawful business activities. If this LLC intends to engage in business activities outside the state of its formation that require the qualification of the LLC in other states, it shall obtain such qualification before engaging in such out-of-state activities.

f. Duration of LLC

The duration of this LLC shall be perpetual. However, this LLC shall terminate when a proposal to dissolve the LLC is adopted by this LLC or when this LLC is otherwise terminated in accordance with law.

2. Management Provisions

a. Management by Manager(s)

This LLC will be managed by the manager(s) listed below.

Name of Manager: Rosa Ruiz

b. Nonliability of Manager(s)

No manager of this LLC shall be personally liable for the expenses, debts, obligations, or liabilities of the LLC, or for claims made against it.

c. Authority and Votes of Manager(s)

Except as otherwise set forth in this agreement, the articles of organization, certificate of organization, or certificate of formation, or under the laws of this state, all management decisions relating to this LLC's business shall be made by its manager. If there is more than one manager of the LLC, management decisions shall be approved by a unanimous vote of the managers, with each manager entitled to cast one vote for or against any matter submitted to the managers for a decision.

d. Term of Manager(s)

A manager may be removed at any time by the member. In addition, each manager will cease to serve upon any of the following events:

- the manager becomes disabled, dies, retires, or otherwise withdraws from management, or
- the manager's term expires, if a term has been designated in other provisions of this agreement.

Upon the happening of any of these events, a new manager may be appointed to replace the departing manager by the member.

If there are no managers in place after a manager is removed or ceases to serve, the member shall be manager until a manager is duly appointed. If there are no managers in place and the member has died or become incapacitated or is unable to act as manager, the member designates Carlos Ruiz as manager until the member or the member's successor is able to act.

e. Manager Commitment to LLC

Manager(s) shall devote his or her best efforts and energy to achieve the business objectives and financial goals of this LLC. By agreeing to serve as a manager for the LLC, the manager agrees not to work for another business or endeavor owned or operated by himself or herself or others, if such other work or efforts would compete with the LLC's business goals, mission, products, or services, or would diminish or impair the manager's ability to provide his or her best efforts to manage the business of this LLC.

f. Compensation of Manager(s)

No manager of this LLC is entitled to any fee for managing the operations of the LLC unless such compensation is approved by the LLC. Managers may work in other capacities for this LLC and may be compensated for performing such additional services, whether as officers, employees, independent contractors, or in other capacities as approved by the LLC.

g. Indemnification of Manager(s)

A manager shall be indemnified by the LLC for any debt, obligation, or other liability, including reasonable attorneys' fees, incurred in the course of the manager's activities or performance of duties on behalf of the LLC as long as the manager complied with the duties of loyalty and care when incurring the debt, obligation, or other liability. This provision does not in any way limit the indemnification the manager would be entitled to under applicable state law. The indemnification provided shall inure to the benefit of successors and assigns of any such manager.

3. Membership Provisions

a. Nonliability of Members

No member of this LLC shall be personally liable for the expenses, debts, obligations, or liabilities of the LLC or for claims made against it.

b. Reimbursement of Expenses

Members are entitled to reimbursement by the LLC for reasonable expenses incurred on behalf of the LLC, including expenses incurred in the formation, dissolution, and liquidation of the LLC.

c. Compensation

A member shall not be paid for performing any duties associated with membership, including management of the LLC. Members may be paid, however, for services rendered in any other capacity for the LLC, whether as an officer, employee, independent contractor, or otherwise, as approved by the LLC.

d. Membership Certificates

This LLC shall be authorized to obtain and issue certificates representing or certifying membership interests in this LLC. Each certificate shall show the name of the LLC and the name of the member, and shall state that the person named is a member of the LLC. The certificate shall entitle the member to all the rights granted members of the LLC under the articles of organization, certificate of organization, or certificate of formation; this operating agreement; and provisions of law. Each membership certificate shall be consecutively numbered and shall include any additional information considered appropriate for inclusion on membership certificates.

In addition to the above information, all membership certificates shall bear a prominent legend on their face or reverse side stating that there are transfer restrictions that apply to membership in this LLC under this operating agreement and shall give instructions for obtaining a copy of these restrictions upon request from this LLC.

The records book of this LLC shall contain a list of the names and addresses of all persons to whom certificates have been issued, show the date of issuance of each certificate, and record the date of all cancellations or transfers of membership certificates by members or the LLC.

e. Membership Action

Except as otherwise may be required by the articles of organization, certificate of organization, or certificate of formation; other provisions of this operating agreement; or under the laws of this state, any required or authorized action by the member on behalf of the LLC may be done by written consent or resolution but such written consent or resolution is not required to authorize action by the member.

f. Admission of New Members

One or more additional persons or entities may be admitted into membership in this LLC as determined by the member. If any new member or members are admitted, this operating agreement shall be amended as appropriate, and, if required, the articles of organization, certificate of organization, or certificate of formation shall also be amended.

Any assignment of an economic interest in the LLC shall not entitle the assignee to voting or management rights in this LLC, and the assignee shall not become a member of the LLC.

4. Tax and Financial Provisions

a. Tax Classification of LLC

This LLC shall be initially classified as a sole proprietorship (disregarded entity) for federal and, if applicable, state income tax purposes. It is understood that the LLC may change its tax treatment by signing, or authorizing the signing of, IRS Form 8832, *Entity Classification Election*, and filing it with the IRS and, if applicable, the state tax department within the prescribed time limits.

b. Tax Year and Accounting Method

The tax year of this LLC shall end on the last day of the month of December. The LLC shall use the cash method of accounting. Both the tax year and the accounting period of the LLC may be changed if the LLC qualifies for such change, and may be effected by the filing of appropriate forms with the IRS and state tax offices.

c. Title to Assets

All personal and real property of this LLC shall be held in the name of the LLC, not in the name of any individual member.

d. Bank Accounts

The LLC shall designate one or more banks or other institutions for the deposit of the funds of the LLC, and shall establish savings, checking, investment, and other such accounts as are reasonable and necessary for its business and investments.

The member and the manager shall have the authority, and the member may designate another person or persons with the authority, to deposit and withdraw funds of the LLC, and to direct the investment of funds from, into, and among such accounts.

The funds of the LLC, however and wherever deposited or invested, shall not be commingled with the personal funds of the LLC member.

5. Capital Provisions

a. Capital Contributions

The member shall make the following contributions of cash, property, or services to the LLC, on or by specified dates, as shown next to the member's name below. The fair market values of items of property or services as agreed between the LLC and the contributing member are also shown below.

Name of member: Rosa Ruiz

Description of contribution:

Cash in the amount of $5,000

Total value of contribution: $5,000

Contribution deadline: January 15, 2017

b. No Interest on Capital Contributions

No interest shall be paid on funds or property contributed as capital to this LLC, or on funds reflected in the capital account of the member.

c. Capital Account Bookkeeping

A capital account may be set up and maintained on the books of the LLC for the member. It shall reflect the member's capital contribution to the LLC, increased by any additional contributions by the member and the member's share of profits in the LLC, decreased by any distributions to the member and the member's share of losses and expenses of the LLC, and adjusted as required in accordance with applicable provisions of the Internal Revenue Code and corresponding income tax regulations.

d. Additional Contributions

The member may contribute additional cash or other assets to the LLC in the member's sole discretion.

e. Allocations of Profits and Losses

Except as otherwise provided in the articles of organization, certificate of organization, or certificate of formation or this operating agreement, the profits and losses of the LLC, and all items of its income, gain, loss, deduction, and credit, shall be allocated to members in accordance with the member's capital interest in this LLC.

f. Allocation and Distribution of Cash

Cash from LLC business operations, as well as cash from a sale or other disposition of LLC capital assets, may be allocated and distributed from time to time as may be decided by the manager(s).

6. Dissolution Provisions

a. Events That Trigger Dissolution of the LLC

The following events shall trigger a dissolution of the LLC:

i. **Expiration of LLC Term.** The expiration of the term of existence of the LLC, if such term is specified in the articles of organization, certificate of organization, or certificate of formation or this operating agreement, shall cause the dissolution of this LLC.

i. **Written Agreement or Consent to Dissolve.** The written agreement or consent of all members to dissolve the LLC shall cause a dissolution of this LLC.

iii. **Entry of Decree.** The entry of a decree of dissolution of the LLC under state law shall cause a dissolution of this LLC.

If the LLC is to dissolve according to any of the above provisions, the member(s) and, if applicable, manager(s), shall wind up the affairs of the LLC, and take other actions appropriate to complete a dissolution of the LLC in accordance with applicable provisions of state law.

b. Dissociation of a Member

The dissociation of a member, which means the death, incapacity, bankruptcy, retirement, resignation, or expulsion of a member, or any other event that terminates the continued membership of a member, shall not cause a dissolution of this LLC. This LLC shall continue its existence and business following such dissociation of a member.

7. General Provisions

a. Officers

The LLC may designate one or more officers, such as a President, Vice President, Secretary, and Treasurer. Persons who fill these positions need not be members of the LLC. Such positions may be compensated or noncompensated according to the nature and extent of the services rendered for the LLC as a part of the duties of each office. Ministerial services only as a part of any officer position will normally not be compensated, such as the performance of officer duties specified in this agreement, but any officer may be reimbursed by the LLC for out-of-pocket expenses paid by the officer in carrying out the duties of his or her office.

b. Records

The LLC shall keep at its principal business address a copy of all proceedings of membership meetings and resolutions, as well as books of account of the LLC's financial transactions. A list of the names and addresses of the current membership of the LLC also shall be maintained at this address, with notations on any transfers of members' interests to nonmembers or persons being admitted into membership in the LLC.

Copies of the LLC's articles of organization, certificate of organization, or certificate of formation; a signed copy of this operating agreement; and the LLC's tax returns for the preceding three tax years shall be kept at the principal business address of the LLC. A statement also shall be kept at this address containing any of the following information that is applicable to this LLC:

- the amount of cash or a description and value of property contributed or agreed to be contributed as capital to the LLC by the member
- a schedule showing when any additional capital contributions are to be made to this LLC by the member
- a statement or schedule, if appropriate, showing the member's right to receive distributions representing a return of part or all of the member's capital contribution, and
- a description of events, or the date, when the legal existence of the LLC will terminate under provisions in the LLC's articles of organization, certificate of organization, or certificate of formation; or this operating agreement.

If one or more of the above items is included or listed in this operating agreement, it will be sufficient to keep a copy of this agreement at the principal business address of the LLC without having to prepare and keep a separate record of such item or items at this address.

c. All Necessary Acts

The members, officers, and managers, if any, of this LLC are authorized to perform all acts necessary to perfect the organization of this LLC and to carry out its business operations expeditiously and efficiently as authorized by this agreement and by law. The secretary of the LLC, or other officers, or its members, may certify to other businesses, financial institutions, and individuals as to the authority of one or more members, officers, or managers, if any, of this LLC to transact specific items of business on behalf of the LLC.

d. Severability

If any provision of this agreement is determined by a court or an arbitrator to be invalid, unenforceable, or otherwise ineffective, that provision shall be severed from the rest of this agreement, and the remaining provisions shall remain in effect and enforceable.

e. Entire Agreement

This operating agreement represents the entire agreement of this LLC, and it shall not be amended, modified, or replaced except by a written instrument executed by the undersigned member or his or her successor as well as any and all additional parties who became members of this LLC after the adoption of this agreement.

8. Signatures of Members and Spouses of Members

a. Execution of Agreement

In witness whereof, the member of this LLC, and all managers on the date of execution of this agreement, sign and adopt this agreement as the Operating Agreement of this LLC and agree to abide by its terms. A person who is both member and manager of this LLC shall sign twice: once in the capacity as member of this LLC and once in the capacity of manager of this LLC.

Date: _____

Signature: _____
Rosa Ruiz, Member

Date: _____

Signature: _____
Rosa Ruiz, Manager

b. Consent of Spouses or Domestic Partners (or Equivalents)

The undersigned is the spouse or domestic partner (or partner to a civil union or reciprocal beneficiary or partner of an equivalent nature) of the above-signed member of this LLC. This spouse (or equivalent) has read this agreement and agrees to be bound by its terms in any matter in which he or she has a financial interest, including restrictions on the transfer of memberships and the terms under which memberships in this LLC may be sold or otherwise transferred.

Date: _____

Signature: _____
[Name of spouse or domestic partner (or equivalent)]
Carlos Ruiz

Resolutions for a Single-Member LLC

Written Consent for Sole Member to Open a
Bank Account and Borrow Money

Written Consent of the Sole Member of
_____[Company name]_____, LLC
A [State] Limited Liability Company

_____[Member's name]_____, who is the sole member of
_____, LLC (the "Company"), in accordance
with the Company's operating agreement, hereby adopts the
following resolutions as if they were adopted at a member meeting.

Resolved, that ____[member's name]_____ is authorized to
open accounts for the Company at any bank, including checking
accounts, savings accounts, and other deposit accounts.

Resolved, that ____[member's name]_____ is authorized
to endorse checks and orders for the payment of money and to
withdraw and transfer funds on deposit with any bank where the
Company has an account.

Resolved, that ____[member's name]_____ is authorized
to establish a line of credit with a bank on behalf of and in the
name of the Company including signing any documents required by
a bank to establish a line of credit.

Resolved, that ____[member's name]_____ is authorized to
borrow money on behalf of and in the name of the Company, and to
sign promissory notes or other evidences of indebtedness on behalf
of the Company.

Dated:_____   _____
                            [Member's Signature]

                            _____
                            [Member's Printed Name], Sole Member

Written Consent Granting Authority to Sole Member to Purchase Real Estate

Written Consent of the Sole Member of
_____[*Company name*]_____, LLC
A [*State*] Limited Liability Company

_____[*Member's name*]_____ , who is the sole member of _____[*company name*]_____ , LLC (the "Company"), in accordance with the Company's operating agreement, hereby adopts the following resolutions as if they were adopted at a member meeting.

Resolved, that the Company wishes to purchase the real property located at: _____[*address*]_____ (the "Property") for the price of $____[*amount*]____ and according to the other terms and conditions provided for in the purchase and sale agreement for the Property.

Resolved, that _____[*member's name*]_____ is authorized to handle all matters related to the purchase of the Property on behalf of the Company, including but not limited to:

- signing any contracts related to purchase of the Property on behalf of and in the name of the Company
- placing money for the purchase of the Property into escrow on behalf of and in the name of the Company
- signing any other documents required to purchase the Property (such as loan documents and insurance documents) on behalf of and in the name of the Company, and
- attending a closing on behalf of and in the name of the Company to complete the purchase of the Property.

Dated:_____   _____
                         [*Member's Signature*]

                         _____
                         [*Member's Printed Name*], Sole Member

Written Consent of Sole Member
Granting Authority to Another Person

Written Consent of the Sole Member of

_____[*Company name*]_____, **LLC**

A [*State*] Limited Liability Company

_____[*Member's Name*]_____, who is the sole member of _____[*company name*]_____ , LLC (the "Company"), in accordance with the Company's operating agreement, hereby adopts the following resolution as if it was adopted at a member meeting.

Resolved, that _____[*person's name*]_____ is hereby granted authority to transact the following business or perform the following tasks on behalf of the Company:

_____

_____

This named person is also granted the authority to perform any incidental tasks necessary to accomplish the primary business or tasks described above.

Dated:_____   _____

[*Member's Signature*]

_____

[*Member's Printed Name*], Sole Member

Written Consent of Sole Member Rescinding Authority

Written Consent of the Sole Member of
_____[Company name]_____, LLC
A [State] Limited Liability Company

_____[Member's Name]_____, who is the sole member of
_____[company name]_____, LLC (the "Company"), in accordance
with the Company's operating agreement, hereby adopts the
following resolution as if it was adopted at a member meeting.

Resolved, that _____[person's name]_____ was granted
authority on _____[date]_____ for the purpose of
transacting the following business or performing the following
tasks on behalf of the Company:

_____

_____

This authorization is no longer deemed necessary for the Company
and any and all authority delegated to this person under the prior
authorization is hereby rescinded and no longer in effect.

Dated:_____   _____
                       [Member's Signature]

                       _____
                       [Member's Printed Name], Sole Member

Written Consent of Sole Member
Delegating Authority to Rent Business Space

Written Consent of the Sole Member of
_____[*Company name*]_____, LLC
A [*State*] Limited Liability Company

_____[*Member's name*]_____, who is the sole member of
_____[*company name*]_____, LLC (the "Company"), in accordance with the Company's operating agreement, hereby adopts the following resolution as if it was adopted at a member meeting.

Resolved, that _____[*person's name*]_____ is authorized to negotiate and sign a lease for office space on behalf of the Company at _____[*property address*]_____ at a monthly rent of $_[*amount*]_ and according to the other terms and conditions provided for in the lease.

Dated:_____   _____
                           [*Member's Signature*]

                           _____
                           [*Member's Printed Name*], Sole Member

Using the Downloadable Forms on the Nolo Website

This book comes with eforms that you can access online at
www.nolo.com/back-of-book/SMLLC.html

To use the files, your computer must have specific software
programs installed. Here is a list of types of files provided by this book,
as well as the software programs you'll need to access them:

- **RTF.** You can open, edit, print, and save these form files with most
  word processing programs such as Microsoft *Word*, Windows
  WordPad, and recent versions of *WordPerfect*.
- **PDF.** You can view these files with Adobe *Reader*, free software
  from www.adobe.com.

Editing RTFs

Here are some general instructions about editing RTF forms in your
word processing program.

- **Underlines.** Underlines indicate where to enter information.
  After filling in the needed text, delete the underline. In most
  word processing programs you can do this by highlighting the
  underlined portion and typing CTRL-U.
- **Bracketed text.** Bracketed text indicates instructions. Be sure to
  remove all instructional text before you finalize your document.
- **Signature lines.** Signature lines should appear on a page with at least
  some text from the document itself.

Every word processing program uses different commands to open,
format, save, and print documents, so refer to your software's help
documents for help using your program. Nolo cannot provide technical
support for questions about how to use your computer or your software.

> **CAUTION**
> In accordance with U.S. copyright laws, the forms provided by this
> book are for your personal use only.

List of Forms Available on the Nolo Website

To access these forms, go to: **www.nolo.com/back-of-book/SMLLC.html**

Form Title	File Name
Sample Operating Agreement for a California Single-Member Limited Liability Company (Manager-Managed)	SampleOperatingAgreement.pdf
Written Consent for Sole Member to Open a Bank Account and Borrow Money	ConsentOpenBankAccount.rtf
Written Consent Granting Authority to Sole Member to Purchase Real Estate	ConsentPurchaseRealEstate.rtf
Written Consent of Sole Member Granting Authority to Another Person	ConsentAnotherPerson.rtf
Written Consent of Sole Member Rescinding Authority	ConsentRescindingAuthority.rtf
Written Consent of Sole Member Delegating Authority to Rent Business Space	ConsentRentBusinessSpace.rtf

Index

●

 **NOLO** *More from Nolo*

Nolo.com offers a large library of legal solutions and forms, created by Nolo's in-house legal editors. These reliable documents can be prepared in minutes.

Create a Document Online

Incorporation. Incorporate your business in any state.

LLC Formation. Gain asset protection and pass-through tax status in any state.

Will. Nolo has helped people make over 2 million wills. Is it time to make or revise yours?

Living Trust (avoid probate). Plan now to save your family the cost, delays, and hassle of probate.

Provisional Patent. Preserve your right to obtain a patent by claiming "patent pending" status.

Download Useful Legal Forms

Nolo.com has hundreds of top quality legal forms available for download:

- bill of sale
- promissory note
- nondisclosure agreement
- LLC operating agreement
- corporate minutes
- commercial lease and sublease
- motor vehicle bill of sale
- consignment agreement
- and many more.

More Bestselling Books

Legal Guide for Starting & Running a Small Business
$39.99

Legal Forms for Starting & Running a Small Business
$29.99

Tax Savvy for Small Business
$29.99

How to Write a Business Plan
$34.99

The Small Business Start-Up Kit
A Step-by-Step Legal Guide
$29.99

Every Nolo title is available in print and for download at Nolo.com.

www.nolo.com

△△ NOLO *Save 15%* off your next order

Register your Nolo purchase, and we'll send you a **coupon for 15% off** your next Nolo.com order!

Nolo.com/customer-support/productregistration

On Nolo.com you'll also find:

Books & Software
Nolo publishes hundreds of great books and software programs for consumers and business owners. Order a copy, or download an ebook version instantly, at Nolo.com.

Online Forms
You can quickly and easily make a will or living trust, form an LLC or corporation, apply for a provisional patent, or make hundreds of other forms—online.

Free Legal Information
Thousands of articles answer common questions about everyday legal issues, including wills, bankruptcy, small business formation, divorce, patents, employment, and much more.

Plain-English Legal Dictionary
Stumped by jargon? Look it up in America's most up-to-date source for definitions of legal terms, free at Nolo.com.

Lawyer Directory
Nolo's consumer-friendly lawyer directory provides in-depth profiles of lawyers all over America. You'll find information you need to choose the right lawyer.

SMLLC2